I0558223

MUGGED by REALITY

When Heavens Resource Meets Human Isolation

Dr. Scott T. Kelso

Holland Robinson Publishing

An imprint of Holland Robinson Publishing / Digging Up Dreams LLC

Fort Worth, Texas 76117

First Published in the United States of America by Holland Robinson Publishing 2023.

Copyright © 2023 by Scott Kelso. All rights reserved.

Holland Robins supports copyright. Copyright fuels the economy of a better world, a creative space to be authentic, and a thriving culture. Thank you for supporting this book, and for complying with copyright laws by not reproducing, scanning, or distributing any part of it in any form without permission.

Book Design and Layout – Boss Media

Paperback ISBN: 978-1-961074-10-1

Unless otherwise noted, Scripture quotations are taken from the Revised Standard Version of the Bible, copyright © 1946, 1952, and 1971 or New Revised Standard Version Bible copyright © 1989 National Council of the Churches of Christ in the United States of America. Used by permission. All rights reserved worldwide.

Endorsements for *Mugged by Reality*

"I am delighted to commend to you this wonderful book by Scott Kelso, *Mugged by Reality*. Scott offers us all a surprising gateway into the spiritual realm by raising our awareness and by unpacking some of the essential but often overlooked keys to Spirit-empowered Christian living to which the Scriptures point us. Scott reminds us that the unseen realm of the Spirit is more real than the everyday earthly realm that we live in. He opens up a charismatic worldview and makes more accessible our opportunity and calling to participate in the advancing of God's Kingdom, which is in us, among us, and in our midst. May we all be inspired and challenged by Scott to cease being spectators in the Kingdom conflict that surrounds us and get in the game as full-on participants."

David Cole
Professor of Historical Theology
The King's University

"Scott Kelso has written a timely book focusing on the reality of the unseen spiritual realm in our lives. It is full of biblical wisdom, personal stories, and insights drawn from his wide experience of Christian ministry. Each chapter explores a particular biblical character and looks at their relevance for us today. Scott's engaging style means that it an easy read but full of hidden gems. This is an excellent book for devotional reading. It will form, and even transform, your walk with God."

Dr. Richard Roberts
Author of *We See in Part: Reframing Prophecy Today*

"Ninety to ninety-five percent of the universe is dark matter or dark energy. That means the vast majority of the universe is invisible. Yet the average educated person in the West would think that angels and demons are a fairytale. There is an invisible world behind the seams of space and time that regularly interacts with our world if we would open our spiritual eyes. Scott Kelso helps to open our eyes and take us for a journey into the spirit world, where the supernatural emerges into our world with signs, wonders, and miracles. He shows us through Scripture and personal testimony how the power of God invades, breaks, and shakes our world to bring the Kingdom of God. Dr. Kelso's writing is clear, fast-moving, and gripping as he invites us to let God get a hold of us and turn our world upside down."

Pete Bellini, Ph.D.
Professor of Church Renewal and Evangelization in the Heisel Chair
Director of Non-Degree Programs
United Theological Seminary
Author of *Thunderstruck: The Deliverance Ministry of John Wesley Today*

"Dr. Scott Kelso is a father to a generation and one who has modeled his new book...*Mugged by Reality*. This revelation is a must-read for a generation that has bought into the false reality of the radical sexual agenda. Scott reveals how to access the unseen world to bring what is unseen into view and to bring light to a dark world, to bring God's purposes for the generation of the Lord's return."

Brondon Mathis
Director, Hope for the Nations
Author of *The Antioch Mandate*

"How is God at work in the world, and how do we make sense of trauma and tragedy? Deeper still, how do we respond to all that swirls around us not in the natural but in the *supernatural*? In *Mugged by Reality*, Scott Kelso invites us to not only wade into these theological waters, but to let ourselves become immersed in the deep things of God. He wants to help us recover our longing, our passion. As a pastor well acquainted with troubled waters, I am grateful for this kind of rich and real spiritual direction."

Rev. Carolyn Moore
Former President Wesley Covenant Association
Mosaic Church
Augusta, GA

"Drawing on the riches of Old Testament examples that still speak to us today, *Mugged by Reality* shows God's miraculous power is neither new nor stamped with an expiration date of sometime in the days of the early church. And God manifests this New-Creation power – heaven's reality — to and through ordinary believers today. Read and believe!"

Mark E. Roberts, PhD
Senior Professor, Bible & Culture
Oral Roberts University, Tulsa, OK, USA

I dedicate this book to all those desiring to "see the Kingdom of God" (Luke 17:20-21) in our day. The Kingdom of God is already here—the invisible made visible through Jesus Christ in you, the Hope of Glory.

FOREWORD

Scott Kelso is a man well aware that we live in two worlds, one seen and one unseen. One temporal and one eternal. One that is fading away and one which shines brighter and brighter until full day (Proverbs 4:18).

Through decades of pastoring, teaching, and offering apostolic leadership to the worldwide Church, Scott has gained insight into God's ways of working behind the scenes of life and history.

It's been said that our lives are like a building with a lower story and an upper story. The lower story is our daily life, with its joys and sorrows and babies and bills and victories and defeats. The upper story, unseen to us, is where God is working out the great purpose of an eternal Kingdom, the big picture of the arc of history. Occasionally, the upper story breaks through to our lower story, and we are mugged by the greater reality. C.S. Lewis said, "Reality is usually something you could not have guessed." Reality surprises us as the eternal invades our experience.

The Bible is, among other things, a wonderful story book. Scott Kelso leads us through a fresh telling of the biblical stories of ten men and women of God. Each of them had times when eternal reality broke through into their human experience, revealing the principles and power of an unseen Kingdom. That breakthrough was sudden and powerful. They felt like they had been "mugged by reality." Scott reveals how the eternal Kingdom principles they learned apply to our lives today.

Be ready. No matter what is happening in the lower story of your life, you're about to be "mugged by reality"!

Dr. John K. Smith

Author of *Rublev's Trinity: An Ancient Painting, An Awesome God, and You*

Contents

Introduction

The most "real" world is the unseen world, hence the title of this book. The apostle Paul says in 2 Cor. 4:18: "We look not at what can be seen but at what cannot be seen; for what can be seen is temporary, but what cannot be seen is eternal" (NRSV). Think of the everyday entities that govern our world: microwaves connecting our cell phones; radio waves carrying all manner of communications, including awesome pictures of distant galaxies in space; sun flares, which are immense energy bursts that can violently affect the weather on earth; and electricity transforming the way we have lived for the last 100 years. All of these are invisible yet real, in fact, as real as anything we can see, smell, taste, touch, or hear.

And so, it is in the spiritual world as well—unseen yet present. Jesus tried to explain it to Nicodemus, a ruler of the Jews who came to Jesus by night. Jesus told him, "The wind blows where it wishes, and you hear the sound of it, but cannot tell where it comes from or where it goes. So is everyone who is born of the Spirit" (John 3:8

NKJV). When the unseen reality of the spiritual world manifests during our journey here on earth, we call it a miracle, a healing, a sign, or wonder. Whatever it is, affects our real-time experience in this world.

In Mark 9:24, a demonized boy is cured. The boy's father brought him to Jesus because the disciples could not heal him. The boy was suffering from a demonic spirit (unseen but real), which caused him to convulse, foaming at the mouth and rolling on the ground, displaying all manner of bizarre behavior. Jesus asked him how long this behavior had been happening, and the father said since childhood—"and it has often cast him into the fire and into the water, to destroy him, but if you can do anything, have pity on us and help us" (Mark 9:22)[1]. "And Jesus said to him, 'If you can! All things are possible to him who believes'" (v.23). "Immediately the father of the child cried out and said, 'I believe; help my unbelief'" (v.24). So, Jesus rebuked the unclean spirit, saying to it, "'You dumb and deaf spirit, I command you, come out of him, and never enter him again'" (v.25). At this point, I am sure the people were amazed, the father was overjoyed, and the disciples were perplexed. Later, the disciples asked Jesus why they could not cast out the spirit. He said, "This kind cannot be driven out by anything but prayer."

My contention in this book is that when the unseen reality of the unseen world manifests in our life experience, it often is dramatic, observable, and leaves us with our jaws dropped open. I believe at that instant, a person "sees things that cannot be unseen." The

---

[1] Unless otherwise noted, all biblical references will be from the Revised Standard Version.

course of their life is altered, never again to be the same. When we encounter the invisible unseen world of the Spirit of God, we are ruined for the ordinary. We are, if you will, "mugged by reality"!

In the chapters that follow, allow me to review biblical characters who were "mugged by reality," people who had their life experience so drastically intercepted by the unseen realm of God that they were forever changed and, in some cases, changed the course of history. For instance, I am confident that the father of the demonized boy mentioned above felt "isolated" or "trapped" in his frustration to see his son healed. After all, his own flesh and blood was completely enslaved to a bizarre demonic spirit, never knowing when it would manifest. Friends, we are living in a day and hour when multitudes feel the same isolation: a wife suffers her husband's death from COVID-19, isolated in a hospital, never having the opportunity to say goodbye or even have a funeral. Or take, for instance, a parent whose teenage daughter takes a harmless pill at a party and dies within minutes of fentanyl poisoning or a subway passenger in New York, patiently waiting for the train to arrive while being cold-cocked by a complete stranger for no reason, perhaps languishing in a coma for days on end or even succumbing to death. How can one explain the horrors of the world we are living in? And yet there is an unseen reality waiting in the wings for those who believe, even if they need help with some unbelief. A comforting scripture I have quoted to myself many, many, times is Psalm 34:7: "The angel of the Lord encamps around those who fear him, and delivers them."

I vividly remember an experience years ago when returning from our Annual Conference in Lakeside, Ohio, and losing control of my vehicle. It was mid-afternoon, and I was traveling south on Interstate 75 just south of Findley, Ohio. I was watching an Army convoy on the berm of the opposite side of the freeway pulling off the road. While being distracted, I ran up to the bumper of the car in front of me. Violently, I jerked the wheel to avoid a collision. My car began to spin out of control. I then proceeded to skid into the median, slide all the way across the grassy median, up onto the incoming traffic going north. As I heard horns blaring and tires screeching, I slid all the way across the highway and stopped on the berm with the Army convoy right in front of me. When I got out of the car, one of the Army officers said, "Son, you sure must have somebody watching over you." Again, Psalm 34:7. The miracle was I never hit anyone, and no one ever hit me or anyone else. No damage at all to anyone. I was "mugged by reality"!

If the Bible says anything, it declares that there is a God in heaven who is not "unable to sympathize with our weakness" (Heb. 4:15). This God loves us with an everlasting love and is prepared to intervene in our isolation and trauma of life. This God knows, cares, and can come to our aid. The following chapters will throw light on such a God as we review the dramatic real-life biographies of some prominent biblical characters who have blazed the trail and set a pattern of hope for all who may be trapped in impossible life experiences.

Furthermore, all this is not to say that we don't have a part in God's unfolding plan for our lives. We have handles. What is your handle? Everyone has some handle that God can grab onto to further your spiritual journey and propel you to significance in the Kingdom of God. Let's review some examples of handles. Moses had his rod, which became a means of activating miracles. David had his slingshot, which took out a giant with one shot. Gideon had a horn to rally the troops, and Sampson with unusual strength used the jawbone of an ass to defeat Israel's enemies. Esther had beauty beyond compare, as well as the counsel of a wise uncle, saving the Jewish people from annihilation. Jehoshaphat had a heart to worship the living God in the face of overwhelming odds and prevailed.

As you read these stories and turn the pages, please know that God has a way of putting us in the right place at the right time as He grabs a hold of one of our handles to advance His purpose on the earth. When we live with expectancy and confidence that our lives are fully in God's control—anything is possible. As the unseen realm hovers over our journey, the possibilities become endless. So, let's journey together and peer at life beyond the veil.

CHAPTER ONE

Job's Battle and Yours

I have chosen to begin with the book of Job in the Old Testament because we all go through perplexing experiences, often attached to traumas, while at the same time leaving unanswerable questions in their wake. This certainly was the case with Job. Most biblical scholars agree that Job's trial only lasted a matter of months in comparison to his whole life. They were, however, power-packed days of trauma, to be sure, and extended to every area of his life—mental, physical, emotional, and spiritual. In the end, Job finally found peace through his relationship with the Creator, as well as material restoration.

For context, let's review the big picture first. The book of Job's opening statement reveals what kind of man Job was. It says, "There was a man in the land of Uz, whose name was Job; and that man was blameless and upright, one who feared God, and turned away from evil." [2] Right out of the gate, the reader realizes that Job had all his ducks in a row. He is not only a man with great integrity; he

---

[2] Job 1:1.

has a wonderful family with sons and daughters, loads of material possessions, and servants to the extent that the author states, "This man was the greatest of all the people of the east."[3] However, with all this to his credit, he is not insulated from life's trauma.

The Plot Thickens

There came a day when God was holding council (Job 1:6) with an elite hierarchy called the "sons of God." In this convention, Satan also came among them. At this moment, most readers of the Bible are baffled. Why is a maligning force known as the Prince of Darkness appearing in the council of the Most High God? How could the enemy of God and the adversary of all goodness ever be given recognition in such an enclave? It really boggles the mind. We are reminded from the words of the prophet Isaiah in chapter 55, "For my thoughts are not your thoughts, neither are your ways my ways, says the Lord."[4] I guess we have to tighten our loins and read on.

Could it be that Satan's attendance at such a council suggests that even he is subject to a superior restraint that can and does set limits on his reach into the human drama? He is not free to pursue all mischievous designs without restraint. He is answerable to God and in the end will get his due. We know from the New Testament that his end is certain—annihilation. However, in this council, Satan makes a request to go after Job. He taunts the Almighty that

[3] Job 1:3b.
[4] Isaiah 55:8.

Job only serves God because of all the blessings God has given him. God gives Satan permission to remove Job's natural blessings, including his children. Job passes the test with his relationship with God still intact. The Bible says, "In all this Job did not sin or charge God with wrong."[5]

We now move to round two. Satan says to God, the only reason why Job has remained faithful is because he has not felt the full throttle of temptation in his physical body. But if Job were to lose his health, then he would curse God. Apparently, God had enough faith in Job to allow even this scenario to manifest. Satan afflicts Job "with loathsome sores from the sole of his feet to the crown of his head."[6] Satan was to stop before death would occur. At this point, even Job's wife said to curse God and die. Wow! This must have been the pits. However, again, the record shows that Job "did not sin with his lips" (2:10). Consequently, Job's friends heard of his predicament and came to console and comfort him. They sat with him for seven days without saying a word. They were speechless as they witnessed the horror of his physical condition.

When Job finally talks after seven days of silence, he admittedly is frustrated and confused. Chapter three says when Job opened his mouth, he said, "Let the day perish wherein I was born, and the night which said, 'a man child is conceived. Let that day be darkness!'"[7] Job continues, "Why did I not die at birth, come forth

---

[5] Job 1:22.
[6] Job 2:7.
[7] Job 3:3.

from the womb and expire?" [8] Agonizingly he continues, "For then, I should have lain down and been quiet; I should have slept; then I should have been at rest." [9]

Digging Deeper

In life's misfortunes, we are called upon to dig deeper for lasting dimensions of meaning as we all look to the unseen reality at hand. Today, we have the advantage of the New Testament revelation and 2000 years of church history to help give perspective. We are in a much better place than Job to negotiate life's trauma in many regards. This, however, does not lessen the sense of misery we all will endure at some point in our journey. We live in a fallen world, awaiting its final release of restoration back to the Creator himself. Until that time, we must war against the same satanic schemes that befell Job. I have always appreciated the Old Testament prophet Habakkuk's take on suffering and heartache. He said:

> "Though the fig trees do not blossom,
>
> nor fruit be on the vines, the produce
>
> of the olive fail and the fields yield no food,
>
> the flock be cut off from the fold and there
>
> be no herd in the stalls, yet, I will rejoice in
>
> the Lord, I will joy in the God of my salvation." [10]

[8] Job 3;11.
[9] Job 3:13.
[10] Habakkuk 3:17-18.

Job's battle typifies a crisis for many people today. His experience with illness, calamity, and heartache was unfair, inexplainable, and exhausting! Why did this have to happen? Let me say that the unexplainable intersects our lives many times before we die. We are left to grapple with sudden disasters, tragedies, and unexplained misfortunes all through our life. I have been in the ministry fifty years, and I have not known one person who has avoided these things. I suppose if we had everything completely explained and laid out before us, we would not need faith. But that is the point of it all. We do need faith. The Bible says without faith, it is impossible to please God.[11] Even the Bible enumerates unexplainable events. Take, for instance, Matthew 2:18 when there was weeping and wailing in Ramah on the death of all the infants killed by King Herod in his search for the baby Jesus. Imagine processing that tragedy! Or in Luke 13, where a tower of Siloam fell and killed eighteen people in a kind of random event. Jesus asked the crowd, "Were these worse offenders than all the others that dwelt in Jerusalem? No, but unless you repent, you will all likewise perish." [12]

In Numbers 16, during Korah's rebellion against Moses and Aaron, the ground opened and swallowed scores of people alive. Think of the plagues of Egypt, directed by Moses using his rod or several other biblical disasters through history. None of this is easy to talk about, but if one does not have some context with the Lord, one can really be left hanging. I remember the great earthquake in 2010 in Haiti. Two hundred thousand people perished, and millions

[11] Hebrews 11:6.
12 Luke 13:14b-15.

were left homeless. The nation is still recovering from that one. Most people cannot even imagine such destruction.

There are biblical answers the reason for suffering. First, God is not happy with the state of the world. It hurts Him as well as us. Isaiah 63:9a says, "In all Israel's affliction He was afflicted." Lamentations 3:33 says, "He does not enjoy hurting people or causing sorrow." And Ezekiel 18:23 states, "Do I take pleasure in the death of the wicked? Declares the sovereign Lord. Rather, am I not pleased when they turn from there ways and live? For I take no pleasure in the death of anyone, declares the sovereign Lord" (NIV). In addition, when Jesus witnessed suffering and disfigurement, He saw a terrible distortion of God's intent for humanity. Jesus spent time healing people to point them toward God's ideal for humanity. Tim Keller makes this statement in his book *The Reason for God*: "If we again ask the question: Why does God allow evil and suffering to continue: and we look at the cross of Jesus, we still do not know what the answer is. However, we know what the answer isn't. It can't be that he doesn't love us. It can't be that he is indifferent or detached from our condition. God takes our misery and suffering so seriously that he was willing to take it on himself." [13]

Secondly, our sin is the cause of much suffering! Psalm 119:67 says, "Before I was afflicted, I went astray; but now I keep thy word." When our lives are integrally related with others, our failing can hurt them as well. Sometimes we are tempted to strike out at God

[13] Timothy Keller, The Reason for God: Belief in an Age of Skepticism (New York, NY: Viking Press, 2008)

in our frustration. Take note of Proverbs 19:3: "When a man's folly brings his way to ruin, his heart rages against the Lord." We want to blame God for the mess we get ourselves in. Some people leave God out of their lives for years at a time. Then, when they find themselves in a jam because of sinful choices, they suddenly become religious and wonder where God has been. What I am trying to say is do not minimize the extreme damage that sin can produce in human relationships. Human suffering is often directly related to human evil.

Finally, the Bible states there can be a redemptive side to suffering. Romans 8:28 says, "We know that in everything God works for good with those who love him, who are called according to his purpose." A college professor once asked her students to write on one side of a sheet of paper the ten worse things that ever happened to them and on the other side the ten best things. Some items were found on both sides. The great Russian dissident Alexander Solzhenitsyn, speaking of the harsh imprisonment in the gulag, said, "I nourish my soul there, and I say with hesitation; Bless you prison, for having been in my life."

The Bible tells us how the brothers of Joseph intended to do evil to him, selling him into slavery, but God took this cruel act and used it to put Joseph in a position years later, where he would end up saving many lives, including the lives of those same brothers. Does this happen in every case of tragedy? Certainly not! But the Scriptures are clear on this: if we give our lives to God and ride out the storm with Him, He will cause everything to work for ultimate good, either in this world or in the world to come.

Now add to this picture an adversary who is hungry to spoil our journey in life, and you will find a toxic tonic indeed. Let's be clear: Job's adversary in his great poem is Satan, not his friends who would not give him a break concerning the reason for his suffering. They kept trying to tell Job that he did something to cause all his tragedy. They were wrong, but they were not the enemy. Job's enemy was Satan. To the Hebrew mind, a name is not just a label. It depicts the character of the person. With respect to Satan, we see his evil work and maligning plans flow together to discredit all God's people up to and through Christ's great victory on the cross, as well as all Christ has accomplished. Please know you and I are in Satan's bullseye. Thank God we have the victory over him because of Jesus.

Job's Opposition and Ours

Satan's name means "accuser" or "slanderer" (Hebrew). The Greek means "diabolos;" the French means "diablo," and the English means "devil." Revelation 12:10 maintains that Satan's constant and unremitting focus is to accuse the saints of God, but they defeat him by the blood of the Lamb and the word of their testimony. In the first two chapters of Job, as we have seen, the "enemy" (another name for Satan in the Bible) is presented as Job's accuser and tormentor. When we read Zechariah 3:1, we see Joshua, the high priest at the time, has a vision of the restoration of God's people following the Babylonian captivity, "with Satan accusing him." In

1 Chronicles 21:1, the "accuser" tempts King David to number the people, to exalt in his military might. This was not authorized by God.

All of history has acknowledged a spiritual duality to explain the light versus dark side of life. Very early in the charter of redemptive history (GER *heilsguchichte*), mankind is acutely aware of a maligning, evil, unrelenting, and opposing force that manifests with persistent pressure. It is as if there is an intelligence rivaling God's authority, a power of concentrated and hateful wickedness with which we are to contend. The Christian often finds himself caught in what I call "suspended frustration" with respect to the area of the dark side of life. We know it is real, as we often feel its affect, yet feel helpless to do much about it. One may feel like a ship on the high seas always subject to the whims of the waves.

Tracking along with this malevolent presence throughout history is also a belief in a good, transcendent, and merciful God who has guided the Judeo-Christian understanding of the world for the last 4000 years. Surprisingly, the Bible has no sustained argument for the existence of God. His existence is a matter of fact from the beginning. The opening words of the Bible are "In the beginning God created the heavens and the earth." [14] The New Testament book of Hebrews says, "And without faith it is impossible to please God, because anyone who comes to him must believe that he exists and that he rewards those who earnestly seek him." [15] The Psalmist

[14] Genesis 1:1.
[15] Hebrews 11:6.

concurs, "The heavens declare the glory of God and the firmament proclaims his handiwork." [16] In addition, "The earth is the Lord's and the fullness thereof, the world and those that dwell therein..." [17] Mankind has observed, not manufactured, the marks of God's design from time immemorial. The existence of such quantitative truth, goodness, beauty, and the uniformity of nature suggest the unseen presence of a Creator/Sustainer.

In summation, the above understanding of the world denotes an incongruent side, an evil force bent on wearing us down. The work of an unholy spirit is evidenced all around us, not to mention the Christian doctrine of God and man's salvation are untenable without the existence of Satan. In other words, one cannot write Satan out of the human story and imagine that the story is unchanged. If we are honest, we see the fruit of man's fallen nature, the self-destructive tendencies of every civilization history have recorded. The prevalence of disease and disorder point to an enemy among us, sowing seeds of destruction. Dare I say COVID-19 is the most recent example and overlaid with political influence, which has served to complicate the entire experience. If we fail to accept and understand this flow of reality, we will never understand our life and its ultimate purpose.

[16] Psalm 19:1.
[17] Psalm 24:1.

Back to the Storyline

Job's experience as he was questioned by his friends was "steady as you go." The cumulative effect of their argument was "Job, you must have done something wrong." Job actually affirms the retributive theology of his day, yet in this instance, he stubbornly maintains his innocence. After several volleys from his friends, he rejects their counsel—they simply did not understand. For Job, his being "mugged by reality" came only after a long slog through some very deep and perplexing waters. "In the debate with the three friends, Job expressed his conviction that his suffering was the result not of his sin but rather, since he suffered despite his innocence, of God's injustice." [18] Job thought if he could confront God directly, however terrifying that may prove to be, he could make his case.

Beginning in Chapter 38, Job gets his wish, but it did not go down well. God properly unbraids Job with a series of questions that only the Almighty Himself could answer:

"Where were you when I laid the foundation of the earth?

Tell me if you have understanding. (38:4)

Who determined its measurements—surely you know!

Or who stretched the line upon it? (38:5)

On what were its bases sunk, or who laid the cornerstone,

When the morning stars sang together, and all the sons of

---

[18] Tremper Longman III, *The Fear of the Lord is Wisdom: A Theological Introduction to Wisdom in Israel* (Grand Rapids, MI: Baker Academic, 2017), 56.

God shouted for joy?" (38:6-7)

Or this—

"Have you commanded the morning since your days begun,

And caused the dawn to know its place? (38:12)

Do you know the time when the mountain goats give birth?

Do you observe the birth pangs of the deer? (39:1)

Can you number the mouths that they fulfil, or

Do you know the time when they bring forth?" (39:2)

This round of questioning ends with God not interested in Job's response or even telling him why he is suffering. Instead, God ends the discussion with these words: "Shall a fault finder contend with the Almighty? He who argues with God, let him answer it." [19] Ouch! From a literary standpoint, we know God is peeved because he begins the section with speaking "out of a whirlwind" (38:1). This is code language for "you have ticked me off."

God begins the second round of questions (not quite as pointed as the first round) with this searching query: "Will you even put me in the wrong? Will you condemn me that you may be justified?" [20] Following this second round of unbraiding, Job finally sees the light. His response is recorded in verses 42:1-6. He confesses that he speaks in ignorance and repents before the Almighty.

---

[19] Job 40:2.
[20] Job 40:8.

Conclusion

Most people think the book of Job is about suffering. "Job famously suffers, but the book's primary issue is not the nature of suffering, for it is not interested in answering questions of why we suffer. No. Job's suffering presents the occasion for raising the real issue of the book: wisdom." [21]

Job states in the twenty-eighth chapter: "Behold the fear of the Lord, that is wisdom; and to depart from evil is understanding." [22] This same reference is mentioned throughout the Old Testament as a bedrock reason for navigating life successfully. It is mentioned throughout the book of Proverbs many times, beginning in Proverbs 1:7. The author of Ecclesiastes (wisdom literature) also ends his entire argument for keeping God at the forefront of one's life with this: "The end of the matter; all has been heard. Fear God and keep his commandments; for this is the whole duty of man." [23]

Where true wisdom is increased, the fear of the Lord is deepened. And that is growth in relationship with God. Toward the end of the story, Job realizes that he is not at fault for his suffering, and God is not asleep at the switch and therefore unjust. God was informing Job that there was more about God that he needed to learn. In other words, "go deeper in God and you will live." This, in fact, is a very important spiritual principle. No matter who you are or what your station in life may be: THERE IS ALWAYS MORE IN GOD.

---

[21] Longman, 43.
[22] Job 28:28.
[23] Ecclesiastes 12:13.

Job was a righteous man who lost everything, including his children. Behind the scenes, completely unknown to Job, God was going to prove to the adversary that people do not merely serve Him because He makes them rich and prosperous. "Remember my life is a breath; my eye will never again see good." [24] Yet there is a lot we don't know when we are in the heat of the battle. It is foolhardy to tell God how to run His universe. However, when the sufferer has a personal encounter with God, the questions give way to the reality of your relationship with God Himself. When I look at Jesus and what He suffered for me, I take refuge in the loving arms of a God who has stepped into my world and says, "I know!" When we see and recognize God for who He is, we don't need all the answers. He is enough! He is the living God.

Finally, we concluded in Job's experience: "And the Lord restored the fortunes of Job, when he had prayed for his friends, and the Lord gave Job twice as much as he had before." [25] Job ended up "mugged by reality." This is consistent with the flow of divine action throughout the Old Testament. [26] God can and does reverse our lot in life. "Blessed is the man who endures trial, for when he has stood the test, he will receive the crown of life which God has promised to those who love him." [27]

When we pursue a relationship with God and stick with it, we not only insulate ourselves from a hopeless destiny; we also have

---

[24] Job 2:2.
[25] Job 42:10.
[26] See Ps. 107:33-36.
[27] James 1:12.

the confidence that the God of the universe has our best interests at heart while He leads and directs the steps of His children all the way home. Sometimes we are so mystified by the destination, we forget about the journey. Pay attention to the journey, then go home. Selah!

CHAPTER TWO

Esther: Appointment with Destiny

Several years ago, a limited showing of a movie entitled *One Night with the King* came to our local theater. It was about the story of Esther in the Bible. Naturally, as a Christian pastor, I encouraged our people to see the movie. Needless to say, the movie generated some good reflection concerning our role and call as believers in contemporary American society.

As you may or may not know, Esther, a beautiful young Jewish female living in exile from her homeland Israel, is being raised by her uncle whose name is Mordecai. She becomes the hero of a story set in ancient Persia under the rulership of King Xerxes (Ahasuerus 486-465 BC), reigning in the city of Susa. His empire stretched from India to Ethiopia, one of the largest the world has ever known.

In the third year of Xerxes's reign, he organized a party to include all the princes, governors, and high military officials. The Bible says, "On the seventh day," the king summoned the queen to come before the banquet and show off her beauty. She refused to follow protocol and was stripped of her position and sent away to live in exile. Sometime later, a search process ensued to find a new queen. A large group of candidates were assembled from the far reaches of the empire. Esther was one of the candidates to be presented to the king following a twelve-month preparatory period. Her preparation included six months of anointing with oil and myrrh and six months with spices and other ointments. When her day came to be presented to the king, she won his heart and became the new queen. Esther not only stepped into a beauty contest, but she unknowingly was summoned by the Lord God to turn history for future generations. She would become a key player in averting a covert attempt to annihilate the Jewish people.

One of the behind-the-scenes lessons as we journey through this story, as well as many other stories we will be covering from the Bible, is that in moving in the will and purpose of God for your life, God is able to place you at the right place, in the right time, or the right reason. We see this in the story of David and Goliath; we see this in the prophet Jonah and Nineveh; and we see this with Gideon and the Philistine confrontation. Please know your life is not a random event. It is given purpose and meaning through the one who created you. Things don't just happen in the life of the sojourner of faith; things happen for a purpose. This should bring comfort to everyone reading these words. You and I are on a journey, and we are going to complete that journey with a sense of satisfaction and awe.[28]

---

[28] See John 17:4.

Let's Dive in Deeper

Esther's uncle Mordecai used to sit among some of the king's officials at the king's gate. It is "likely he held some kind of office in the Persian complex at Susa." [29] At one point, he became aware of a plot to harm the king, a kind of inside job. Mordecai told Esther, and Esther told the king. There was an investigation, and it was found to be true. Danger was averted. Concurrently, the king appointed a man named Haman, the villain of the story, to be over all the princes. This was a very high position, a kind of head of state. In this position, all other officials were ordered to bow down to Haman as he passed by. Mordecai would not bow down, probably because he discerned a moral perversity in Haman. You see, Haman was a descendent of the Amalekites, who were bitter enemies of the Jews. As a result, Haman was enraged at the insubordination of Mordecai and ordered the annihilation of all the Jews throughout the empire. As a personal observation, it seems to me, only a madman would initiate such an evil plot to avenge such a small infraction. After all, he was not the king.

Mordecai tips off his niece to the evil intent of Haman and urges her to go before the king and intercede. He also asks her and others to fast toward this effort. An interesting detail at this point in the book of Esther is it is the only book of the Bible that does not mention the name of God. However, as one commentator has said, "The absence of the name of God does not mean the absence

---

[29] Gregory A. Lint, Executive Editor, *The Complete Biblical Library: Ezra-Job (Springfield, IL: World Library Press*, Inc., 1995), 277.

of the hand of God." [30] Most people who know anything about the Judeo-Christian faith know that fasting is attended with prayer, and prayer assumes a relationship to a "higher power," i.e., God. So even though God's name is not mentioned in the story, His fingerprints are all over it! In fact, "more space is devoted in rabbinic literature to commentary on Esther than another work in the Bible besides Genesis." [31] Fasting and prayer are part of the outworking of God's plan for our lives.

At this point in the story, Mordecai exhorts Esther as to her call in life—"For if you keep silence at such a time as this, relief and deliverance will rise for the Jews from another quarter, but you and your father's house will perish. And who knows whether you have not come to the Kingdom for such a time as this?" [32] In other words, she was at the right place at the right time, for the right reason. She was appointed by destiny to save the Jews from a hellish plot to exterminate them from history.

Furthermore, Esther finds herself in a real quagmire. No one could approach the king unless he held forth the golden scepter. To go in unannounced would normally mean certain death. However, Esther was a goner either way, because when the king would find out she was Jewish, she also would go down with the ship. Esther knew she had to confront the king. The stakes were too high. Her

---

[30] Merrill C. *Tenney, Zondervan Pictorial Encyclopedia of the Bible,* Vol.2, D-G (Grand Rapids, MI: Zondervan Publishing House, 1975), 380.

[31] Yoram Hazony, *God and Politics in Esther* (Cambridge, United Kingdom: Cambridge University Press, 2016), 209.

[32] Esther 4:14.

moment of greatest fear became her moment of greatest destiny. Esther was about to get "mugged by reality."

Application

Fast forward twenty-five centuries. There are many ways we could go with this timeless story, but I am haunted by similarities between Esther's day and ours. I say this because, in some respects, there is a movement afloat in the West with particular emphasis in America to bring a kind of annihilation to God's people in contemporary society. No, I am not talking about someone actually killing Christians, of course, but rather rendering them ineffective by silencing their voice in the culture, relegating them only to the four walls of the church building. Hear this: there is a spirit assigned from hell to this generation to slowly strangle their voice, their reputation, and their influence on the Christian story in our society. Much of this is being spearheaded by those who hold an elitist view in key positions in education, government, and the media.

It is no secret there is an ever-widening rift by the day between what we call the sacred and the secular throughout our culture. The word secular comes from the Latin word "sacularis," which literally means "of or relating to the world." By and large, the word carries a negative connotation for Christian believers because if something is of a secular nature, then it does not relate to the supernatural, to religion, or to the church. I want to say over the last one hundred years, the worldview of secularism has gained a gigantic hold on the minds of people in the Western world. This touches every area of modern life but is especially keen in the political realm. Richard John Neuhaus wrote a very probing and widely read book on this subject in 1984 entitled *The Naked Public Square*. His thesis was: the naked public square is the result of political doctrine and practice that would exclude religion and religiously grounded values from the conduct of public business. [33]

The success of this "secular creep" for the most part has divided the world into two dramatically opposed belief systems: the sacred and the secular. The secular, broadly defined, "is the view that all of reality is physical, consisting of some configuration of matter and energy, and that everything that exists either currently has a scientific explanation or will have a scientific explanation in the future." [34] If this assessment of the secular is true, one could surmise a movement afoot to annihilate the sacred and remove it from any working function in our society. I know it sounds bazar, but I believe it is the case in present day America. Furthermore, as I reflect on Esther, I wonder if we, the Christian church, have not come to the kingdom for such a time as this. Collectively, as a people group, we Christians still hold the trump card for our society. But it is fading fast.

I suppose the sacred and the secular have always been somewhat at odds. They are two different worlds. But at times, worlds collide,

---

[33] Richard John Neuhaus, *The Naked Public Square: Religion and Democracy in America* (Grand Rapids, Mi: Wm. B. Eerdmans Publishing House, 1985), IX.

[34] Brendan Sweetman, Why Politics Needs Religion: *The Place of Religious Arguments in the Public Square* (Downers Grove, Il.: IVP Academic, 2006), 17.

and someone has to pick up the pieces. Charles Taylor, a well-known professor of philosophy, wrote an 850-page book on the subject some fifteen years ago. In it, he declares that until the modern era, political organization throughout society, any society "was in some way connected to, based on, guaranteed by some faith in, or adherence to God."[35] Along with modernity comes the fragmentation of the larger society and a falling off religious belief and practice. This has progressed to the point in the twenty-first century that belief in God is "no longer axiomatic."[36] Belief in God is one of many options.

In light of the above cultural condition, the people of God (the church) find themselves at a real tipping point in the modern world. We must understand we are not at war with people. We are at war with ideas, ideologies, philosophies, and concepts that guide civilization. We cannot afford to take God out of the mix, as Europe has done. Do you know that when the leaders of the European Union prepared a new European Constitution in 2003, the document contained no reference to God or the Christian heritage? Can you imagine just erasing 1300 years of history as if it never happened? Many believe the same type of mindset is coming our way. In fact, it is here.

[35] Charles Taylor, *A Secular Age (Cambridge, MA.: the Belknap Press of Harvard University Press, 2007)*, 1.
[36] Ibid., 3.

Synthesis

As we continue to think of Esther's life and ours, several things have come to mind. Let's look at a few strategic ones before we close out this chapter.

First, as believing Christians, we are royalty. Like Esther, we have attained royalty when we accepted Christ as our Savior and Lord, becoming children of the God of the universe. We were not born with this privilege. It came to us through the invitation of Christ. We were chosen.[37]

Esther also was chosen. As she became part of the royal household, she gained power, prestige, all the things that accompany the throne of a royal household. But they were not hers to grasp. She had a higher purpose over enriched living, satisfaction, fine food and clothing, security, and all the rest. The throne was not for her personal enjoyment. There was a calling to fulfill—a calling to step into her destiny. God took a hold of her "handle" and moved her into place of strategic importance. And she knew it. She even made the statement as she darkened the doors of the king's chambers— "If I perish, I perish."

At this point, perhaps we should ask God about our "handle." What is the unique thing in our lives that the Lord wants to use to further His kingdom in these turbulent days? The apostle Peter tells the Christians in the diaspora: "Judgment begins with the

---

[37] See 1 Peter 2:5ff.

household of God."[38] Our nation is under indictment. The national sins of America have reached a peak. According to the word of God, there are four things that summon judgement for a nation: a) when violence overtakes a nation[39]; b) when gross sexual acts become common and accepted[40]; c) when the land becomes polluted because of the blood of the innocent crying out from the ground[41]; d) when the hearts of God's people turn to idols.[42] All these and more we have seen come to the fore in one generation.

As a result, a description is unpleasant at best. Our society is in chaos in many respects. The criminals have more rights than innocent victims. The English language is being redefined as we speak with new words to accommodate sexual perversion and gender fluidity.[43] Our southern border is wide open with millions coming in illegally every year. Divorce and ravaged families have become the norm of the day. Psalm 91:5 comes to mind: "You will not fear the terror of the night, nor the arrow that flies by day, nor

---

[38] 1 Peter 4:17.

[39] Proverbs 1:18-19; Isaiah 63:3-4.

[40] Genesis 19:24; Leviticus 18:22-23; Ezekiel 16:50-52.

[41] Proverbs 16:17; Exodus 21:22; Leviticus 18:21; Deuteronomy 24:16.

[42] Jeremiah 16:18; Ezekiel 37:23.

[43] The Horn News.com, Dec. 22, 2022: "Stanford University announced a full 13 pages of un-woke words it wants to eradicate from our vocabulary, from popular use, and from the dictionary. It all began last May 20, when the university began the Elimination of Harmful Language Initiative (EHLI). The EHLI is a multi-phase, multi-year project to address harmful language such as: 'beat a dead horse' and 'kill two birds with one stone' are eliminated because they 'normalize violence against animals.'" "You can't call a group of people 'guys' because 'this term reinforces male-dominated language'---but you can't call a whole group of women 'ladies' either, because it 'lumps a group of people using gender binary language that doesn't include everyone.'" Frank Holmes reporting.

the pestilence that stalks in darkness." The arrow could be a nuclear threat and the pestilence could be COVID-19 or worse. And to boot, the vilest sins one can mention are in the church, not only in the secular culture. God has a controversy with us, and we have not yet come to see it. Our enemy is not the Supreme Court, the Congress, or even the devil. It is God who has a controversy with us and we have failed to discern it. We need apostles and prophets to step up to the plate and spell it out for us, or we will perish.

Secondly, we have history on our side. As God's people, we are to stand and point others to the way of freedom. There are so many in bondage, just waiting for someone to tell them, "Here is the way; walk in it!" God's people have been in tight places before, but almost always, they find a path of deliverance and a way to make God's name great.

Several years ago, I took a thirteen-week course on world missions called Perspectives on World Missions. One of the resource authors was a man named Steve Hawthorne. Steve explained there are three understandings with respect to the name of God in Scripture. The first is God's name tag name, where the function is reference. These names identify our God and place Him in a category all His own. Some examples are Yahweh, Elohim, Lord of Hosts, and Almighty.[44] Secondly, there are God's window names, where the function is revelation. An example would be "The Lord is my shepherd; I shall not want" (Ps. 23). I follow Him around. He tends the sheep, protects the sheep, and provides for the sheep. Other names in this

---

[44] See 2 Samuel 7:18-19: where Lord God is Adonai-Yahweh. (rare)

category could be Creator or Redeemer. The third category and the one that supports this section of my argument is God's fame name, where the function is God's global namesake. In this category, God's historical incidents establishes His worthy reputation. For instance, most occurrences of the phrase: "His name," "My name's sake," and "call upon the name of the Lord" are purpose phrases and common not referring to any particular name tag name. It is like the entire bundle of truth He has revealed through His fame name.

Actually, God left His name unpronounceable: we have consonants, but we do not have the vowels, e.g., YHWH—"I am that I am" or "I cause to be what I cause to be." Something out of nothing. How can you even track something like this? Well, we watch for His footprint in history with people like Abraham, Moses, David, and Esther. The bundle of His renown names equals His fame name.[45]

The third synthesis point I want to make is we have a call from God to defend and propagate the faith. We are not the only generation to battle the anti-Christ spirit. Thankfully, God has given us many tools that former generations did not possess to further His name in the earth. We have the Holy Spirit inside us to empower us in the call (Acts 1:8). We also have the unity of the believing world purchased by the blood of Jesus.[46]

In addition, God chose us for the task of standing up and standing firm for the truth of the Gospel. Also, Ephesians 2:10

---

[45] See Jeremiah 16:21; Isaiah 12:4; Psalm 96:5-6, 8, 10; Psalm 89:14-18; 1 Kings 18:24.

[46] See Ephesians 2:13-16; 1 John 1:7; 1 Peter 2:9.

[47] See 2 Thessalonians 2:13 (NIV).

declares we are His handiwork created for good works, to produce a visible witness for the Lord as we walk in our journey. He chose us from the foundations of the world. No weapon formed against us will prosper. The devil's attacks come to dissuade us from accomplishing our purpose.

We can only do this way of life if we stay close to God. I believe holiness is the clarion call of God for the church in a last-days environment. God calls us to come out from among them and be holy.[48] Love not the world.[49] Don't settle for the trivial; go for the gold. Many in the church have been reduced to go after the same things the heathen go after, e.g., hedge against inflation, stockpile food, etc. These can become diversions to spend our strength on things that will not last.[50] Fidelity with the world is enmity with God. Our sins will bring us down. It is just too costly. Keep your accounts short with God. And remember God would not have His people in fear. Anytime an angel shows up in the Bible, the first thing out of the angel's mouth is "Fear not!" We got this. Like Esther of old, let's do this life with God as the final chapter of world history ends. It is our time. We are designed for these days. Keep your appointment with God.

Fourthly, and finally, we have the full revelation of Jesus and the Holy Spirit. The anointing that goes along with these two is tremendous. Hear the words of John the Apostle: "The anointing

---

[48] See 2 Cor. 17-18.
[49] See 1 John 2:28-29.
[50] See Ezekiel 7:19.

which you received from him abides in you, and you have no need that any one should teach you; as his anointing teaches you about everything, and is true, and is no lie, just as it has taught you, abide in him."[51] The anointing is the leg up we need to carry the name of Jesus to the ends of the earth.

Actually, the last disciple to die following Jesus was John the Revelator. The book of Revelation is John's handiwork and Jesus's last words to the world. It details in other worldly imagery the things that will come upon the world during the closing hours of history. It is a prophecy, and prophecy is history in advance. Each one of us would do well to acquaint ourselves with the book of Revelation; it is a roadmap to the closing days on the earth. But again, we were designed for these days. If you have been called of God, you will be equipped to fulfill that call.

Concluding Thoughts

Esther did confront the king with the dastardly plot of Haman. The king did respond, and Haman was eventually hung on the same gallows that he prepared for Mordecai. Mordecai was promoted to the position that Haman held in the royal court, and the Jewish people were saved from annihilation. A national Jewish commemoration was created called Purim to forever keep the lesson of deliverance before the Jewish people.[52]

As I muse on Esther's experience, I am reminded of Psalm 25:9:

---

[51] 1 John 2:27-28. Also, John 16:13-14.
[52] See Esther 9:20-22; 32.

"He leads the humble in what is right and teaches the humble his way." God places a heavy regard for humility in both the Old and the New Testaments. It allowed Esther to prevail when the stakes were huge. And it will do the same with us in the twenty-first century. Psalm 18:27 says, "For thou dost deliver a humble people; but the haughty eyes thou dost bring down." And James 4:6 says, "God opposes the proud but gives grace to the humble." May we all swim in this grace as we offer the Lord our "handle" and move in our appointed destiny.

CHAPTER THREE

Daniel:
Living Among Lions

aniel in the lion's den is a story that almost every primary age Sunday School student has heard for the last 250 years. Chapter six in the book of Daniel details the account. In the story, the old Babylonian kingdom was in transition, and Daniel was serving under a Mede ruler named Darius. He was again given much favor and promoted to a high level. The Bible says he "distinguished himself above all the other presidents and satraps because an excellent spirit was in him and the king planned to appoint him over the whole kingdom.[53]

Who was Daniel? Well, to appreciate Daniel's dilemma, we must start at the beginning. Because of the unfaithfulness in Israel's track record, and as a result of prophetic declaration, God judged the nation of Israel in 587 BC. God summoned the powerful heathen nation of Babylon to conquer Israel and carry off her citizens to its foreign boundaries in ancient Mesopotamia (modern-day Iraq).

---

[53] Daniel 6:3.

Daniel was among the first wave of people transported to Babylon in 605 BC. They took the elite rulers and leaders first, a kind of "cream of the crop" group to be indoctrinated to the Babylonian culture, using their gifts for the benefit of the state. The record says, "Then the king commanded Ashpenaz, his chief eunuch, to bring some of the people of Israel, both of the royal family and of the nobility, youth without blemish, handsome and skillful in all wisdom, endowed with knowledge, understanding, learning, and competent to serve in the king's palace and to teach them the letters of language of the Chaldeans."[54]

Daniel exceeded qualifications for this assignment. In today's vernacular, we would say Daniel had the goods. The indoctrination for Daniel and his three friends, Shadrach, Meshach, and Abednego, included three years of intensive enculturation, eating their foods, drinking their wine, dressing in their clothes, and learning all their ways of living. At the end of three years, they were to be brought before the king. The Bible says, "But Daniel resolved that he would not defile himself with the king's rich food, or with the wine which he drank."[55] So Daniel proposed a test (not a toast) to be allowed his Hebrew diet for ten days and see if he was "better in appearance" and physically astute beyond his Babylonian counterparts.

Daniel passed the cultural accommodation test with flying colors, but not without some creative maneuvering. There will always be those who will try to get you to compromise your God

---

[54] Daniel 1:34.
[55] Daniel 1:8.

and your faith in this world. When this happens, we must know two things; we must know who we are, and we must know whose we are. When we know these two things, we will always know what to do.

It becomes apparent from Daniel's life and many others throughout Scripture that God wants us to rise above the circumstances of life and to outshine those who don't have a covenant with God. In other words, we are to live a life of distinction.[56] If the spirit is extraordinary, the mind and the body will follow. All our creativity and ingenuity will flow to God and be used for His glory. He wants to make His name great in the earth—to "outshine" all the other gods. It is the spirit that shapes our life. Jesus said, "The words I have spoken to you are spirit and life."[57] Daniel's life was exemplary. They could not make a Babylonian out of him, hard as they tried. They even changed Daniel's name to Belteshazzar, which means "Bel—protect his life." Bel was the chief god of the Babylonian. Daniel's name meant "God is my Judge."

Author John Lennox tells us, "Name changing was no innocent action. It was an early attempt at social engineering, with the objective of obliterating inconvenient distinctions and homogenizing people so that they would be easier to control."[58] It

---

[56] God told the Israelites early: "And the Lord will make you the head and not the tail, and you shall tend upward only, and not downward; if you obey the commandments of the Lord your God, which I command you this day, being careful to do them, and if you do not turn aside from any of the words, which I command you this day, to the right hand or to the left, to go after other gods to serve them." Deuteronomy 28:13.

[57] John 6:63.

[58] John C. Lennox, Against the Flow: *The Inspiration of Daniel in an Age of Relativism* (Oxford, England: Monarch Books, 2015), 46-47.

was not unusual for a conqueror to assert his authority by changing names of the conquered.

However, Daniel would have not it. Instead, he tapped into what was available to him in God. Because of his covenant with God, he knew he was to rule circumstances and not be ruled by them. In good theological Hebrew form, he was the head, not the tail. This was even confirmed again in chapter six: "Then this Daniel became distinguished above all the other presidents and satraps, because an excellent spirit was in him; and the king planned to set him over the whole kingdom."[59]

Faced with the Lions

Daniel's success in the eyes of the king did not sit well with the other officials. Jealousy set in, and a scheme was devised to trap Daniel in his own religious devotion. These airheads convinced the king to sign an edict forbidding all citizens for thirty days to avoid any petition to any god or name other than Darius, or they would be cast into the den of lions. One can be sure the schemes never cease. There will always be those who display a caustic challenge to righteous rule. History is full of it. Daniel's adversaries tricked the king in a shrewd move to bolster his self-esteem and consolidate his power. We have just seen the equivalent a few years ago in America, only in reverse with the Russian collusion hoax and Donald Trump. The whole thing was fabricated to bring down a sitting president

[59] Daniel 6:3.

because of jealousy, envy, and rage. Thankfully, it all backfired and was proven to be totally false.

In Daniel's case, the spurious petition could not be revoked. It stood ratified according to the law of the Medes and the Persians. However, it seemed like a valid idea to Darius at the time, so he commissioned them to draw up the document. Meanwhile Daniel was aware of the document, yet he continued his daily regimen of prayer in full sight of the others, giving thanks to his God in daily devotion.

With this document in hand, Daniel's opponents believed they were certain of victory. Since Daniel's faith was non-negotiable, he sat by his open window and prayed for all to see. "What happens next implies that Darius saw in Daniel's amazing survival an indication that there was a law higher even than the law of the Medes and Persians, the law of God, and that when they clashed, the latter was to be obeyed."[60] However, the document at hand could not be reversed. The king had no choice but to activate the penalty—into the den of lions you go! I find it interesting at this point in the drama, the king actually retires to his quarters to fast for Daniel all night.

When morning came, the king made haste to the place of execution calling out to Daniel with a loud voice—"has your God been able to deliver you" (Daniel 6:20)? Daniel answered, "My God has sent his angel and shut the lions' mouths and they have not hurt

---

[60] Lennox, p. 209.

me; because I was found blameless before him; and also before you, O king, I have done nothing wrong" (v.22). Daniel was "mugged by reality"! The unseen realm had manifested, and the presence of angels saved the day. In fact, when the king realized what had taken place, he went after the perpetrators. He threw them and their families into the lion's den, and this time, there were no angels to save them. Only a hearty meal for the lions.

Angels on Assignment

Angels appear close to 300 times throughout the Bible and far more than references to Satan or demons. Principally, they are "God's messengers whose chief business was to carry out His orders in the world."[61] John Calvin, the great Reformation theologian, says in volume one of his *Institutes*, "Angels are the dispensers and administrators of the divine beneficence toward us. They regard our safety, undertake our defense, direct our ways, and exercise a constant solicitude that no evil befall us."[62] As God opens our eyes to the constant resources He has provided for all who turn to Him in strength, we will find the way to navigate this life from birth to glory. Psalm 91 reminds us, "For he will give his angels charge of you to guard you in all your ways."[63] And in sequence, "The angel of the Lord encamps around those who fear him, and he delivers them."[64]

---

[61] Billy Graham, Angels: God's Secret Agents (Garden City, New York: Doubleday, 1975), 18.

[62] John Calvin, Calvin's Institutes: Book One, XIV, 9, 11 (Grand Rapids, MI: Associated Publishers and Authors Inc. 1972), 79-79.

[63] Psalm 91:11.

[64] Psalm 34:7 (NIV).

One can track the presence of angels in the book of Daniel at several points. For example, in chapter three, a fourth person (image) is seen in the fiery furnace; chapter five displays the mysterious "finger" writing on the wall during a great royal feast; chapter six, as we have seen, the angels appear to close the mouths of the lions; and in chapter ten, angels are visibly descending from heaven. Angels are not always visible, yet they become visible when necessary. They are a magnificent created spirit being doing the bidding of God in the earth. Upon reading Billy Graham's book on angels years ago, I was amazed at how many times angels surface in Scripture. I read the Bible straight through each year at a pace of three chapters a day, and I noticed angels appear now and then. However, the composite picture blows your mind. They are everywhere throughout Scripture. Amazing!

So, Daniel and his three friends continue to walk in the grace of God and fulfill their calling in ancient Babylonia. Their part in the long drama of God through history is preserved for all to read. Yes, and we can track these events in history because of times, dates, places, and names of historical figures well known. We too must know that the grace of God is available to us in our "hard places." Sometimes being "mugged by reality" is more than being delivered from a tight place; it also is about making a statement on God's glorious superintending of His creation, as we will see in some of the following chapters.

Synthesis

To tie a bow on the experience of Daniel, we need to look at one more concept: FAVOR. The story records, "And God gave Daniel favor and compassion in the sight of the chief of the eunuchs."[65] Someone said, "If you have God's favor, it is the only credential you will ever need." This is a searching thought. What exactly is God's favor? Some theologians would say it is the good will and generosity of a beneficent God who desires to condescend to man to be present with him in life circumstances. It is that inclination of God to intercede on our behalf; one who stays vigilant for our good will, and who can work out the details when we are not. The fact is our God is always on the job—"behold he who keeps Israel will neither slumber nor sleep."[66] Only God can bridge the gap; only God can intervene; only God can work out the details when we cannot.

Furthermore, I find it interesting that favor is used interchangeably with the word GRACE in the New Testament. The only New Testament book without an author's name has some very important things to say about grace. The author begins by saying, "Let us be grateful for receiving a kingdom that cannot be shaken."[67] And again, "Let us have grace whereby we may serve God acceptably with reverence and godly fear: for our God is a consuming fire."[68]

---

[65] Daniel 1:9.
[66] Psalm 121:4.
[67] Hebrews 12:28.
[68] Hebrews 12:29. (KJV)

Grace empowers us to purify ourselves from that which we could not purify ourselves otherwise.

In addition, grace is more the "fire insurance"—granting us entrance into heaven. Without grace, I will revert to one of two religious postures. I will either become an inwardly hypocritical legalist (taking one strict way by living inwardly and secretly in a different manner), or I will be so loosie-goosy that God's grace covers all my sin, even to the point of continuing to practice sin in my life while I presume on God's forgiveness. And so, our ungodly and lustful behavior is excused because no one could really live like Jesus anyway. However, that is exactly why we need grace. Like Daniel, grace will allow us to stand out as lights in the world. The apostle Paul would chime in here and say, "We beg you who have received God's grace not to let it be wasted....so then, let us purify ourselves from everything that makes body and soul unclean, and let us be completely holy." [69] And must we remember this also in the mix: "My grace is all you need, for my power is greatest when you are weak."[70]

I am reminded of Jesus' baptism recorded in Matthew 3:23. When Jesus presented himself to John the Baptist, John said, "I need to be baptized by you." If we fail to recognize our need in the face of pure mercy and grace, we will not prevail in our spiritual journey. God has nothing for the person who has no need. Are you aware of your need for God? I hope so. I certainly am. I could not

---

[69] 2 Corinthians 6:1. (TEV)
[70] 2 Corinthians 12:9. (TEV)

have made it through forty years of ministry without going back to the well over and over again. Do you know that only 10% of those who enter ministry as a profession ever cross the finish line? Some 90% fall away, quit, backslide, give up, chase the dollar because of being conditioned by low income, commit sexual infidelity, and more. It is impossible to prevail without the grace of God.

Speaking again of favor, this gift seems to continuingly follow those who are humble. Proverbs 3:34 says, "Toward the scorners he is scornful, but to the humble he shows favor." And again, in Proverbs 14:9, "God scorns the wicked, but the upright enjoy his favor." Finally in Proverbs 22:1, "A good name is to be chosen rather than great riches, and favor is better than silver or gold." Indeed, the Psalmist is well aware of this gift:

> Psalm 30:5: "For his anger is but for a moment, and his favor is for a lifetime."

> Psalm 89:15-16: "Blessed are the people who know the festal shout, who walk, O Lord, in the light of thy countenance, who exalt in thy name all the day, and extol thy righteousness. For thou art the glory of their strength; by thy favor our horn is exalted."

> Psalm 119:58: "I entreat thy favor with all my heart; be gracious to me according to thy promises."

> Psalm 90:17: "May the favor of the Lord God rest upon us; establish the work of our hands for us, yes, establish the work of our hands."

I am sure Daniel was aware of this one: "I know you are pleased with me, for my enemy does not triumph over me."[71] When favor is present, one is aware of the intervention of God in their affairs.

Final Thoughts on Favor

In the Bible, those who are mentioned to have God's favor are not necessarily persons who experience easy sailing in life. In fact, it is quite the opposite. This has been verified by Daniel's experience, as well as his three friends. Let's look at some other examples in the biblical story to substantiate this fact. For example, Noah found favor with God (Genesis 6:8). His was the ability to hear God in the midst of a wicked and perverse generation; one that God said, "That every imagination of the thoughts of his heart was only evil continually."[72] In such an atmosphere for a very long time (120 years), Noah was ridiculed while he built a boat in a place where there was no water. Yet that boat saved Noah and his extended family, allowing them to repopulate the entire ancient world following the flood. Genesis 6:9 says, "Noah walked with God." There is a huge difference between walking with God and merely living. Those who experience the favor of God walk with God.

Then there is Joseph, who "found favor in his sight and attended him, and he made him overseer of his house and put him in charge of all that he had."[73] The 'he" and "him" in this description is

---

[71] Psalm 41:11.
[72] Genesis 6:5.
[73] Genesis 39:4.

Pharoah, the top dog in ancient Egypt and one of the most powerful men in the world. With God's favor, prosperity comes to all Egypt. Amazingly, Joseph was aware that God was with him, so much so that he attributed to God both his earlier imprisonment and slavery as well as his rise to power.[74]

Next is King David, where it is recorded in Acts 7:46, "who found favor with God." His was not an easy journey: being betrayed by a paranoid king (Saul) who would stop at nothing to vent his jealousy. David had to resort to living in a cave and eating from the fields to stay alive while being pursued by Saul. And all this just for being loyal to his country and his king.

We have already covered Esther and Job, who also fell into the category of God's favor. Concerning Esther, the record says, "The king loved Esther more than all the women, and she found grace and favor in his sight more than all the virgins."[75] And, of course, Job is right there with her. We read, "You have granted me life and favor, and your providence has preserved my spirit."[76]

Finally, there is Mary, the mother of Jesus, who when the angel of God announced her pregnancy said, "Hail, O favored one, the Lord is with you."[77] Mary, only a teenager, young and tender, found herself pregnant and out of wedlock, was told the child within her was called holy. Please remember Mary's culture was not as forgiving

---

[74] See Genesis 45:7-8.
[75] Esther 2:17.
[76] Job 10:12. (Amplified)
[77] Luke 1:28.

as ours today in this regard. Today, if you are pregnant and out of wedlock, it is no big deal, unless you are the one pregnant. But in Mary's Israel, it was a very serious offense. If Joseph, her intended, had not been visited by an angel of God, he would have for sure cut her loose.

Mary's son was born, and his name was Jesus, recognized by Luke in the New Testament with this statement: "And Jesus increased in wisdom and in stature, and in favor with God and man."[78] Of course, Jesus lived his life preaching God's Word, only to have his life end in betrayal, desertion, and death on a cross for a crime he didn't commit. Yet Jesus became the greatest source of favor and blessing the world had ever known. It's true: if you have God's favor, it is the only credential you will ever need.

Conclusion

All the people mentioned above finished their course better than they started. In fact, Ecclesiastes says, "Finishing is better than starting."[79] How we finish is more important than how we begin. To finish well, one must live well. It includes possessing a "relentless" spirit—a spirit of never give up. So, "lift up your tired heads, then, and strengthen your trembling knees. Keep walking on straight paths... Guard turning back from the grace of God."[80] As God's children, we should desperately want to finish well. Let's not turn

[78] Luke 2:52.
[79] Ecclesiastes 7:8. (NLT)
[80] Hebrews 12:15. (TEV)

back from the grace of God, putting up our oars and drifting with the current of the world system. Like Daniel, let's stay above the fray with our conscience intact, and "run the race that is set before us." Finishing is better than starting.

CHAPTER FOUR

Elijah
Choose You This Day!

The prophet Elijah is a huge presence in the Old Testament and a significant prophetic voice in ancient Israel. His persona is quoted several times throughout the Bible and extends well into the New Testament. In fact, the last Old Testament prophet, Malachi, foretold that Elijah would appear again prior to the great Day of the Lord.[81] In addition, it was prophesied that John the Baptist would go before the Lord "in the Spirit and power of Elijah."[82] During the episode of the Transfiguration of Jesus, Peter suggested they build three tabernacles to enshrine worship, one of which would be for Elijah.[83] Finally, Elijah is prefigured as one of the two witnesses of Revelation, chapter eleven, even being raised from the dead. Perhaps the little chorus is appropriate as we study the life of this great prophet:

---

[81] Malachi 4:5. The term "the Day of the Lord' is used many times in the books of Isaiah, Joel, and Zephaniah to describe the end of history and the coming judgement of the Lord of history.

[82] Luke 1:17.

[83] Matthew 17:4.

"Elijah's God still lives today

To take the guilt of sin away;

And when I pray my heart's desire,

Upon my soul he sends the fire." [84]

In this chapter, I have chosen to unpack the story of Elijah and the confrontation with the prophets of Baal in 1 Kings 18. Following three years without rain, the Lord directs Elijah to present himself before Ahab, the King of Israel. While he was traveling to his destination, Elijah encounters Obadiah, who was one of the king's household stewards, and told him to inform the king that he was coming. When he finally meets the king, Ahab greets him with this phrase: "it is you, you troubler of Israel!"[85] Elijah's response is significant: "I have not troubled Israel; but you have, and your father's house, because you have forsaken the commandments of the Lord and followed the Baals."[86]

It is helpful to understand that Elijah had previously commanded the rain to stop in Israel, hoping it would get Ahab's attention—galvanizing repentance and a change of life. You see, Ahab's father, whose name was Omri, had struck an alliance with the Phoenicians, which involved commercial and military ties, as well as state-sponsored religious syncretism.[87] This involved dragging the nation

---

[84] Herbert Lockyer, All the Books of the Bible; *A Combination of Bible Study and Daily Meditation* (Grand Rapids, MI: Zondervan Publishing House, 1986), 87.

[85] 1 Kings 18:17.

[86] 1 Kings 18:18.

[87] See the NRSV Cultural Backgrounds Study Bible (Grand Rapids, MI: Zondervan Publishing, 2019), 606.

of Israel through the foreign gods thing to secure the alliance. Israel was weakened, compromising her uniqueness in the ancient world as a monotheistic nation. Meanwhile, Elijah was used as a prophetic voice to secure their attention to this sin. It had not rained for three and a half years, and that did get the king's attention, but still no repentance. In light of these events, Elijah proposes a showdown with Ahab on the issue of Ahab's persistence in sin, leading the nation down a dark hole of judgement and death.

The Showdown

Here is what the showdown would look like. Elijah proposed for Ahab to gather his 450 prophets of Baal and his 400 prophets of Asherah for a kind of contest on Mt. Carmel. They were both to offer up a meat sacrifice to see whose god would show up and consume the sacrifice by fire. This becomes one of the most dramatic scenes of the Old Testament. I have been to Israel five times and have stood on this very spot. It is quite breathtaking. To the west, one can see the Mediterranean Sea in the distance, and to the east, the great plane of Esdraelon (Jezreel), where many battles have been fought throughout history. There was a source of water nearby and dry wood for the sacrifice.

In the ensuing showdown, it was determined that Ahab's prophets would go first. Of course, their efforts proved futile. After hours of calling on their gods, pleading with their gods even to the point of dancing around the sacrifice and cutting themselves to placate the deities, they remained only a bloody, silent, embarrassed lot. Their gods must have been occupied in other pursuits because they sure didn't show up on Mt. Carmel.

Now it was Elijah's turn. He has no one on his side of the equation. Talk about isolation, wow. Elijah places the carcass of his animal sacrifice on the wood platform. He then digs a trench around the site and begins to soak the entire surface with several jars of water, drenching the sacrifice and filling the trench with water around it as well. Such a visual display would be imbedded in the minds of all who were present. Now Elijah calls upon the name of the Lord. God supernaturally answers by fire, consuming the offering, the wood, the altar, and the water around the altar—gone! Elijah was "mugged by reality." The false prophets were seized and put to death by the river Kishon, near the confrontation site. One needs to get somewhere quiet and read the entire account to receive the full effect. It is quite dramatic.

To me, the most haunting verse in the entire chapter is verse 21:

"And Elijah came near to all the people and said, how long will

you go limping with two different opinions? If the Lord (Yahweh) is God

(Elohim), follow him; but if Baal is God (Elohim), then follow him. And

the people did not answer a word."

Choice and Free Will

The fact is that God created us with the capacity to respond, to make choices, to decide. All of life is determined by the choices we make from the time we wake up in the morning to the time we lay down our head at night. This is simply built into the fabric of creation. The record of our life is set in place by the choices we make. Otherwise, there would be no such thing as a biography! In addition, some choices carry greater consequences than others. The choice to be a follower of God is one such consequence. Elijah knew this and proceeded to present the gathering at Mt. Carmel with such a choice. Only in this instance, it was either monotheism or death.

The stand-off at Mt. Carmel presents us with a similar scenario in our everyday life, albeit not as dramatic. Following God becomes a true either/or daily experience. No fence sitting here. You are either on one side or the other. Take, for instance, how we align with almost any cultural issue today: sexuality, abortion, race, the media, gun ownership and a host of others. The choice surrounding these issues for the most part is binary. One finds themselves on either one side or the other. There is little meeting in the middle.

Our choices translate into action, and our actions forge a destiny. If I superimpose the picture of Mt. Carmel on today's church, it may go something like this: "If the Christ of scripture be the true savior, then surrender to him; if the Christ of modern Christendom[88] supplies your guide, then follow it." The dichotomy in the above statement manifests all around us primarily in modern-day denominational expressions. Most denominations are not governed by tight allegiance to scriptural mandates. An example would be our modern concept of sexuality, where homosexuality is embraced as one of many sexual options. All the major denominations now embrace homosexual practice. The Bible is clear on homosexual expression, but somehow, it gets a pass in the modern world by much of the church.

Prior to the confrontation on Mt. Carmel, Elijah asks; "How long will you go limping between two different opinions?" The word "limping" connotes a divided heart and is well established throughout Scripture.[89] The ancient Hebrews knew from the Law that Jehovah required an "undivided heart."[90] Jehovah was their Father.[91] Yet King Ahab wanted to "combine the worship of Jehovah and Baal, and not to assume a hostile attitude towards Jehovah by the worship of Baal."[92]

---

[88] Christendom was a medieval concept that has governed human commerce for a very long time. At its core, Christendom manifests as a widely practiced cultural ethic based in religious affiliation (Christian) which would transcend any loyalty to state or government.

[89] See Psalm 119:113; James 1:8.

[90] Deuteronomy 6:4-5.

[91] See Exodus 3:15-16. *The name means self-existent, omnipotent, immutable, and Eternal Being: the only God besides whom there is none else.*

[92] Keil and Delitzsch, Old Testament Commentaries: Judges 6:33 to Ezra, (Grand Rapids, MI: Associated Publishers and Authors, 1971), 708.

My denominational affiliation has always been Methodist. I believe it is hard to beat Wesleyan theology. On the issue of free will, Wesley was unambiguous. In a letter to his father, John Wesley reflected on the nature of free will, which is the only "possible and satisfactory account of the origin of evil.[93] He goes on to say that by this power we are "enabled to choose or refuse, and to determine ourselves to action accordingly."[94] This seems to me to argue that action follows decision.

Wesley says in an additional essay on "Predestination Calmly Considered," "I assert, that there is a measure of free-will supernaturally restored to ever man, together with that supernatural light which 'enlightens every man that cometh into the world.'" [95] In other words, through the agency of the Holy Spirit, we have the capacity to decide and to act, hopefully in accordance with the will of God. I believe that "light" is Jesus, as well as the written Word of God.

Dramatic Intervention

I suppose at Mr. Carmel, in a more primitive atmosphere, it took a dramatic visible event to turn the hearts of the people to the Living God. What would it take in our day to do the same? I am talking about a real manifestation whereby the people fall down and say, "The Lord, He is God; the Lord, He is God!" Perhaps some

---

[93] John Wesley, Wesley's Works: Letters Vol.12 (Grand Rapids, MI: Baker Book House, 1978), 2.
[94] Ibid.
[95] Wesley, Works, 10:230.

combination of disaster and miracle would help the scenario along. I would not speculate, of course, but there are some things taking place on our watch that do galvanize the attention of the entire world. Perhaps we could look at a few.

The airplanes that hit the Twin Towers in New York on 9/11 is an example. The entire world stopped to watch the event unfold. People did turn to the Lord, but it was rather short lived. A recent example is that of the Buffalo Bills safety Damar Hamlin, who encountered a routine tackle on Monday Night Football, January 2, 2023. The game was delayed, then cancelled altogether while thousands of people sat stunned, many praying in huddled groups all over the stadium in Cincinnati, Ohio. Meanwhile, Hamlin lay on the ground with his heart stopped. Through television, Facebook, and the Internet, millions of people were made aware of what was happening and began to pray for this man. Nothing quite like it had ever happened in professional or college football in America.

After being rushed to the hospital and put on life support, the nation continued to pray for Damar's healing and restoration. By the end of the week, Damar came out of his coma and asked: "Who won the game?" This became a stunning example of a dramatic intervention of God. I believe it was in response to the combined prayers of millions of people. These kinds of events have the potential to reverberate across the spectrum—"The Lord, He is God; the Lord, He is God!" Nine days later, on January 11, Damar was released from the hospital and taken back to his home in Buffalo. Shortly following this, he went home to recover. Get ready, my friends, because this is only a prelude to what we will all see as we move toward the end of history.

Could We be at a Crossroads in America?

I want to take a few pages and transition from ancient Israel to modern-day America. Many people are asking how can we curb the ethical and moral plunge downward which we have experienced as a society since the 1960s. My past book, *Theological Violence in the 21st Century*, is an attempt to address this very question. Like in Elijah's day, the nation can only spurn the living God so long without colliding with serious consequences. Even now, America is experiencing the tremors of a judgment from God. COVID-19 really upset the apple cart. Millions have lost their steady employment, never to re-enter the job market. The economy is teetering on collapse, even though the government will never tell you the truth.

In this mix, one can track a deflection from traditional values since the 1960s. We live among those who have deliberately engineered a purposed and focused initiative to change the entire landscape of our Judeo-Christian underpinnings. Some of these people have been educators, some politicians, some the media and Hollywood, and I am sorry to say the clergy in many quarters. And yet, America is still the envy of the world. Migrants are crossing our southern border by the millions to have a chance to live in a free nation and prosper. Others are going through the process and becoming legal citizens as a deliberate choice. But what are we offering them to envy? After all, our streets are full of crime, our government is full of corruption, our economy is full of greed, and our hearts are full of evil. What a legacy.

The point is this: do we really like the way America is going, and what can be done about it? Elijah is not going to show up on Mt. Rushmore and challenge the powers that be. Let me suggest three possible scenarios. The first scenario is, I suppose the people could eventually rise up and demand change because of the condition of our society and the present philosophy which has informed it. In our lifetime, we have witnessed mass uprisings in Eastern Europe and Russia which have changed entire continents. I doubt this will happen in America, but it is possible. Somehow, as pathetic as things are in many quarters of our society, we still are not yet desperate for change. In fact, we have a kind of sick accommodation to irrationality and irrational behavior in our society. Our present administration in Washington tells us that our border is secure, and we continue to make wonderful strides forward on illegal immigration. Ridiculous! We have become resigned to a society full of crime, and confusion, and darkness.

A second scenario is that we could experience a real true heaven-sent revival which could crush the deluge of darkness upon us. This happened in Uganda following the death of Idi Amin. Revival is linked to God's sovereign purposes, but the church is tied in here also, at the point of prayer and seeking God for a holy visitation. It seems to me by and large that the church is nowhere near hungry enough to pray this in. Continuing, a third possibility in all of this is that out of the destabilization that takes place in a society following true judgment, a partial revival can occur. There is no question that our nation is heading toward a sure and swift judgment from the hand of God. In the midst of darkness and despair, people will turn to God. How broad will be the turning, no one really knows. We do know God's heart is for repentance and restoration always, and the church must lead the way. If the bottom falls out of America, God will have the church be there to offer true hope.

Free Will Still Matters

I want to encourage us that the exercise of our choice still carries much weight, not only in society, but in the heavenly realms as well. Proverbs reminds us to "guard the heart, for out of it come the issues of life." [96] The word for heart in the Old Testament means "the place where the decisions are made." You see, it is the place where we make choices that the issues of life really come into view. One can see our choices actually forge our destiny. Guard the heart!

In addition, God is calling us each day to choose to live for Jesus. As we read Joshua 24:19-25, we find Joshua put before the people of his day a great choice. That choice was to serve the Lord day by day or to yield to the heathen idols in the land they were possessing. Joshua reminds his generation: "As for me and my household, we will serve the Lord." [97] Again, as we have said earlier, there is a binary choice. We are either a conscript in the army of the Lord, or we will be used by the enemy to work against the Lord. One

[96] Proverbs 4:23.
[97] Joshua 24:15.

does not have to be particularly bent toward evil to work evil. The example of Peter with Jesus can be noted here. Jesus found Peter in a compromising posture when Peter urged Jesus to avoid going to Jerusalem and dying on a cross. At that point, Jesus turned to Peter and said, "Get behind me, Satan." Jesus was acknowledging that when Peter was willing to take the low road of compromise, he was really being used by Satan. It appears much of the church today is already in the hands of the enemy because they have taken the low road of compromise. May God deliver us from such things.

I say all of this because in a day when there is an attempt to erase every vestige of religious influence in the public square, it will in the end be the church, God's church who decides the battle. All the strategies of the enemy come to naught and are foiled when the church decides to walk in her birthright. We are here for one reason and one reason only, to maintain and enforce that which God purchased at Calvary 2000 years ago. We are here to occupy until He comes.

As we conclude this chapter, I believe it is essential for all reading these words to check the foundation or their lives. Read and reread Matthew, chapter seven, where Jesus encourages us to build our lives on the solid foundation Rock, which is Himself. If we build on any other foundation, that foundation will be destroyed, and our lives will come crumbling down. Our choice will determine where we land when the hammer falls. There will be no scurrying around to make last-minute tasks. When the crunch comes, the only thing that will count is your foundation. Take note and build only on the foundation of Jesus. Someone said you never get a second chance to make a first impression. Every choice in these dark days leaves some kind of impression on the landscape of our lives. Value them well and make them right.

CHAPTER FIVE

Moses in Midian:
When Life Makes No Sense

The great historical figure Moses is a study in the ups and downs, the ins and outs of following God. Actually, Moses didn't decide to follow God—he was recruited. Moses was floating in a basket and placed in the Nile River as a baby. Pharaoh's daughter was bathing in the Nile one day and discovered little Moses and saved him to her household. After being raised Egyptian, Moses become a very influential steward in the household of Pharaoh.

One day while making his rounds, Moses saw an Egyptian official abusing a Hebrew slave. Moses, filled with anger, killed the Egyptian and buried his body in the sand. Several days later, Moses observed two Hebrews fighting, so he decided to intervene, and one of the men said, "Who made you ruler and judge over us? Are you thinking of killing us as you killed the Egyptian?"[98] Frightened that word had gotten out about his murder of the Egyptian, Moses fled Egypt and landed in Midian, "isolated" on the backside of the

---

[98] Exodus 2:14.

desert. The priest of Midian, whose name was Jethro, had seven daughters, and Moses eventually married one. Her name was Zipporah.

Now, here is where the story has a cataclysmic turn of events. One day, Moses is tending the flock of Jethro, his father-in-law, near a mountain called Horeb (later to be referred to as Sinai). Moses notices a bush burning in flames of fire—but not being consumed. As he went closer to check it out, a voice came from the burning bush: "Moses, Moses." Here again, we see an angelic being portrayed in an important life narrative. The first thing the angel said to Moses was: "Remove your sandals, for the ground you are standing on is holy" (sacred space). A conversation ensues, and God asks Moses to go back to Egypt and deliver Hebrew people out of bondage. An extended conversation results in Moses being recruited for one of the pivotal events in history—the birth of the Nation of Israel. Moses asks God; "Who shall I say sent me?—a perfectly reasonable question. God says, "I am sent you." The name in Hebrew is Yahweh. It means "I am that I am."

Someone has said, "What God asks me to do never ends with what God asks me to do." Moses can vouch for that! Moses responds to the request of Yahweh and departs for Egypt with his brother Aaron to confront Pharaoh. Again, this becomes pivotal in the history of God's people and the story of redemption in the Bible. Moses uses his newly calibrated staff to work a series of miracles over multiple weeks and months, which convinces Pharaoh to let the people go. These supernatural manifestations included:

turning the Nile River into blood, releasing in sequence a plague of frogs, gnats, flies; plagues of boils on livestock; plagues of hail and locusts; darkness, and finally the death of all first-born human and livestock in Egypt. During all the plagues, the Hebrew people were spared.[99] Now, that is amazing!

The Finger of God

The first two miracles by Moses were duplicated by the magicians of Pharaoh.[100] However, when the third miracle occurred, the plague of gnats, the magicians ran out of tricks. They could not reproduce. In fact, they admitted, "This is the finger of God." I want to take a few lines to unpack this curious phrase in the Bible.

The phrase "the finger of God" is used all through the Bible. After considerable study, I believe it has two basic meanings. First, it is a method used by God to project Himself into the natural realm, while at the same time revealing Himself to us.[101] It serves as a kind of "WOW, you have my attention, God." The Lord God breaks into our realm in a dramatic way. Secondly, the phrase signals a method of convincing mankind of the validity of the message and the messenger.

For the ancient Egyptian, the concept of the "finger" of a deity represented something dangerous and powerful that could bring

---

[99] See Exodus 8:23; 9:4, 26; 10:23.
[100] They were the staff turning to a snake and the water turning to blood.
[101] See Exodus 8:10; 9:16.

about good or evil.[102] There was a familiarity in the ancient world for such a phenomenon. We see in Exodus 31:18 that the stone tablets which Moses received from God on Mt. Sinai were written with "the finger of God." Again, God is projecting Himself into the natural realm while revealing Himself to the new Hebrew nation. It was called the Covenant at Sinai or the Ten Commandments. The idea here is without commitment (covenant), there can be no real focus or direction, security, or longevity in life. This is why marriage in the Bible is called a covenant.

Additional examples of the "finger of God" can be found in Psalm 8:3: "When I look at the heavens, the work of thy fingers, the moon and the stars which thou hast established"—the Psalmist directly attributes the creation to the marvelous intervening power of God. Who among us has not stood before a starlit night and gazed into the heavens, and now with the JWST[103], knowing its endless parameter, or stood at the break of day and seen a fiery red horizon explode on a morning sky? These things shout unspeakable glory all from the "finger of God." They represent everyday miracles set before us. There is something about a miracle that settles the issue at hand.[104]

In the same Psalm, David, taking note of God's handiwork, also observes we are included at the highest level of creation. God has not created us to be a spectator in His grandiose scheme of creation,

---

[102] *See the NRSV Cultural Backgrounds Study Bible* (Grand Rapids, MI: Zondervan Publishing, 2019), 124.
[103] James Web Space Telescope.
[104] See Exodus 10:2.

ever wondering what our place is or where we fit in. Instead, we find that the whole creative enterprise was made for our benefit:

> "What is man that thou art mindful of him,
>
> And the son of man that thou dost care for him?
>
> Yet thou hast made him little less than God,
>
> And dost crown him with glory and honor.
>
> Thou hast given him dominion over the works of thy hands;
>
> Thou hast put all things under his feet."[105]

I don't know about you, but I am ready to take my sandals off! Yes, it is by the "finger of God" that God reveals himself to us, and I might add, unless God does reveal Himself to us, we are lost, groping in the dark with only our inadequate five senses to understand it all.

A second use of the phrase "the finger of God" is to convince mankind of the validity of the message of God: redemption. In the story at hand, God delivers and redeems the Hebrew people from bondage in Egypt. In the New Testament, Jesus, God's Son, has come to redeem us from our sins and restore us to His kingdom. In addition, in the New Testament, "the finger of God" becomes even more focused. It's almost like God is poking His finger in our chest while speaking to us. Take, for instance, Luke 11:20, where a demon was cast out of an individual who was mute. When the person begins to speak words and sentences, the people were amazed.

---

[105] Psalm 8:4-6.

Jesus said: "If it is by the finger of God that I cast out demons, then the Kingdom of God has come to you." It's like in your face: "there you are healed and don't you forget it!"

Another example is found in John 8:16, where Jesus encounters a woman taken in adultery. He proceeds to write something in the sand in coming to her defense. We don't know what He wrote; however, it convinced her accusers to back off. The Bible says they left, one by one. Since it was His finger writing in the sand, it was the "finger of God." And finally, in Psalm 144:1, we find these words: "Blessed be the Lord, my rock, who trains my hands for war, and my fingers for battle." As we project ourselves into the spiritual arena, anointed by God and convinced He will move, the world takes note. By signs and wonders, we can participate in the "greater things" ministry of Jesus and do miracles. [106]

The Straw that Broke the Camel's Back

As we continue with the narrative story in Exodus, we see the final judgment of God on Pharaoh is the one that breaks the back of his stubborn resistance. God sends a waring angel to take the life of all the firstborn in Egypt, "from the firstborn of Pharaoh who sat on the throne to the firstborn of the captive who was in the dungeon; and all the firstborn of the cattle."[107] This was the last straw. Pharaoh relented and let the people go. The Bible says they left in mass: about 600,000 men plus women and children,

---

[106] See John 14:12-13.
[107] Exodus 12:29.

livestock, housewares, silver, and gold all. They were heading for Mt. Sinai to have a festival with the Lord.

In the interim, Pharaoh had a change of mind and decided to pursue the Hebrews with a vengeance. Meanwhile, the Hebrews confront a challenge—the Red Sea. It stops them in their tracks. Now what? The Egyptians still in pursuit and are catching up to the Hebrews with a state-of-the-art army. After speaking to God about this matter, Moses takes his staff and holds it over the water, and the Red Sea parts so Israel can cross over and remain alive. You guessed it. Moses and the people of God were "mugged by reality." The entire company of people made it safely to the other side, while the Egyptian army was in hot pursuit. However, when they arrived in the middle of the separation of waters, the Lord God shut down the miracle, and the entire army drowned in view of the Hebrew nation. This became one of the great miracles of history still reverberating today among the Jewish people who live within the national boundaries of Israel, as well as the rest of the world. They commemorate this event with one of their most holy days: Passover. Four thousand years later and the world is still being impacted from this "finger of God."

The Inhibiting Factor, Then and Now

One of the stock realities of the human condition is that we find a way to complain about many things in life. In this story, the Hebrew people complain at the edge of the Red Sea because they were inconvenienced by a little water; they complained at the edge of Mt. Sinai because of being out in the middle of nowhere with no food; they complained for the next forty years in the desert until a new generation of Hebrews could be prepped to finally go into the Holy Land and take possession. It astounds me considering their recent miracles that this great company of people could complain and give Moses such a hard time. I want to camp here for a moment to look at this baffling problem.

God tells the people His reason for bringing them out of bondage. The explanation is found in Exodus 19:1-5:

"And Moses went up to God, and the Lord called to him out of the mountain, saying, 'Thus you shall say to the house of Jacob, and tell the people of Israel: You have seen what I did to the Egyptians, and how I bore you on eagles' wings and brought you to myself. Now therefore, if you will obey my voice and keep my covenant, you shall be my own possession among all peoples; for all the earth is mine, and you shall be to me a kingdom of priests and a holy nation. These are the words which you shall speak to the children of Israel.'"[108]

God was calling to Himself a people, a voice, a demonstration of who He was and what He would be like so the people of the ancient world could know the one true creator God. They could once and for all rid themselves of their false gods and handcrafted idols and

---

[108] Exodus 19:3-6.

come to the true God. The intention of God was to make the entire nation of Israel a priesthood—leading the people of the world to the true and living God. The problem was, Israel did not fulfill their part of the bargain. I believe "complaining" was their downfall.

I have also noticed complaining has become a regular staple of American life. As Americans, we live in the greatest country in the world with foundational documents that ensure our freedom of expression, freedom of religious preference, freedom to assemble and speak. And yet, it never seems good enough. This same attitude has bled into the church and has all but caused us to freeze our witness to Christ. We live like kings compared to most of the world, but somehow, it isn't good enough. The complaining attitude among the Hebrew people in Exodus caused God to let the entire lot perish in the wilderness. In essence, God had to start all over with another generation to fulfill His plan to acquire the Promised Land. Complaining is that deadly. It obstructs vision, inhibits forward movement, and like a virus, contaminates those around it.

Here is a thought which may cause you to take notice. The early church was free of the virus of complaining. Why? They certainly had no primrose path in life. They lived under one of the most brutal regimes in history. The apostle Paul gave his life after being held in prison in Rome for over two years. The apostle Peter was crucified upside down because he felt he wasn't worthy to be crucified like Jesus. Others were beheaded, burned, sawed in two, or crucified. Stephen, the first martyr of the new church, was stoned to death. By and large, many of the leaders for the first few hundred years of

Christian history met terrible deaths, yet maintained their witness to the faith.[109]

I believe these people had something we don't have. You might be surprised. I am not talking about the Holy Spirit; I am not talking about Scripture. And I am not talking about inside information that would elevate them above others. No, instead, these early Christians were free from the incessant, faultfinding, victimization mentality even though the going gets tough. They were convinced God was in control no matter what it looked like state-side. They knew God was working out His good pleasure in the lives of the faithful regardless of circumstances.[110]

If we are going to prevail in the dark days looming over an end-times church, then we must reject the unscriptural habit of saying, "Well, this is pleasant; it must be God." While at the same time, we say, "Well, this is unpleasant; God must not be in this." It's all or nothing, friends. You either belong to God or you don't. And if you don't, you probably are the cause of most of your problems anyway. And if you do, you can't lose despite your problems.[111] So, the questions we may ask in the bewildering experiences of life is not why, but what. What are you saying to me, God, as I walk my path of life? What is it You want to teach me on this runaway train?

---

[109] See Hebrews 11:32-40.
[110] See Romans 8:28-36. We have it on paper; they had it in their heart.
[111] Colossians 1:27b.

God has forever gone on record as living with us in all pains of life.[112] We turn and see that lonely, twisted, tortured figure on the cross: nails through His hands and feet, back lacerated, limbs wrenched, brow bleeding into his eyes, mouth dry as sand—plunged into God-forsaken darkness. And to add to this horrible scene, Jesus was deserted by His disciples, forsaken by all but a few. He laid aside His immunity to pain. He entered our world of flesh and blood and death. Because of His suffering, our suffering becomes manageable. Because of His Resurrection, our resurrection is assured. He calls us to turn from the corruption of this world and the passion of the flesh and turn to Him. Now, that's the God for me!

Final Thoughts

Moses started out elevated as far as worldly standards were concerned. He was raised in the lap of luxury in the grandest country on earth at the time. But then something happened to change his trajectory. At first, it seemed really strange, becoming a shepherd on the backside of the desert "isolated" from most of humanity. However, in following God, our lives can take many turns along the way. The apostle Paul said, "I have learned, in whatever state I am, to be content. I know how to be abased, and I know how to abound; in any and all circumstances I have learned the secret of facing plenty and hunger, abundance and want. I can do all things in him who strengthens me."[113] Even though our circumstances may

---

[112] Hebrews 2:18 says, *"For because he himself has suffered and been tempted, he is able to help those who are tempted."*
[113] Philippians 4:11-13.

change, our relationship with God does not have to change. We are to weather all conditions and phases of life. The calling to follow God may very well include life at each end of the spectrum. The main thing is to keep our focus and heart for God.

Finally, the author of Hebrews, speaking of Moses, says; "By faith he left Egypt, not fearing the king's anger, he persevered because he saw him who is invisible."[114] Friends, the unseen realm wins again!

[114] Hebrews 11:27. (NIV)

CHAPTER SIX

Abraham:
The Conscience of Character

Following the primeval history (pre-history) of Genesis chapters 1-11, Abraham bursts on the scene receiving a dramatic "prophetic" word from God Almighty, a word which tilts the trajectory of the Bible and history heavenward. It is hard to overemphasize the impact of the word given to Abraham in Genesis 12:1-3. But before we read that Scripture, allow me to say a few words about Abraham.

Abraham is a pivotal person in all of Scripture. He dominates the Old Testament as an anchor of biblical faith, giving context to Israel's understanding of herself, as well as providing a father figure for New Testament faith. In fact, Abraham is mentioned seventy-three times in the New Testament, more than any other Old Testament figure. He lives in the city of Ur of the Chaldees, a southern Mesopotamian city on the east side of the Euphrates River, almost where it empties into the Persian Gulf. Ur was very close to the modern-day city of Basra, an oil depot for the Iraqi government.[115]

Abraham lived in a polytheistic world where ancient religions were birthed, and idols made with hands were worshipped. When the Lord God calls and commissions Abraham, he is a wealthy established figure in the community with a large family and financial means. All this becomes important as we unpack the details of this story. The monumental word in Genesis 12 has tentacles that reach all the way into the twenty-first century. It is a word from God. We need to take a few minutes to break down this word because of its blanket of influence.

The Commission

"Now the Lord said to Abram,[116] 'Go from your

country and your kindred and your father's

house to the land that I will show you.

And I will make of you a great nation, and I

will bless you, and make your name great, so

that you will be a blessing. I will bless those

who bless you, and him who curses you I

will curse; and by you will all the families

of the earth shall bless themselves.'"[117]

---

[115] Everett L. Fullam, How to Walk with God (Nashville, TN; Oliver Nelson Books, 1987), 22.
[116] I have chosen to use the name Abraham, as God changed his name in Genesis 17:5.
[117] Genesis 12:1-3.

Abraham is called to leave his homeland, the familiar trappings of his culture and life, to move to a distant land yet to be revealed. As he does this, God is going to use him to explode into a great nation and to become a blessing to the nations of the ancient world.

I can relate in a sense to this "call" because there was a time in my life when a prophetic word came to me which detailed a traveling and speaking ministry filling my calendar as a local pastor. This traveling ministry would take me around the state of Ohio, across the nation, and even around the world to preach the Gospel of Christ. God has a sense of humor because at the time of my prophetic word, I could barely keep my head above the water in a small country church of 100 people, let alone travel the world. However, this word was confirmed four years later by a powerful prophetic evangelist speaking at my church in May 1984, and literally the next week, my phone began to ring with invitations to preach.[118] The rest, as they say, is history!

An interesting point I want us to see in all of this is the fact that the covenant is activated in the going. Remember the ten lepers who came to Jesus to be healed in Luke 17? The Bible says as Jesus spoke to them from a distance, He said, "Go show yourselves to the priests." The very next sentence says, "As they went, they were cleansed."[119] As we respond to the Word, it activates the plan of God for our lives. I believe this is exactly how it happened with Abraham.

---

118 The complete word is given in my book, *Biblical Eldership: Back to the Future with Spirit-Filled Leadership in the Local Church* (Tulsa, Ok: Word & Spirit Press, 2016.).
119 Luke 17:14.

Breaking Down the Word

The commission given by God to Abraham is far reaching indeed. It involves land, progeny, a religious posture unique in the ancient world, and heavenward blessing. First, the land. Since the God of the Bible is sovereign and the creator of our world, He knew every inch of land mass available. For sovereign purposes, He chose the southern Levant, which runs parallel to the Mediterranean Sea on the east, to the modern-day country of Jordon on the west, to the border of today's Lebanon to the north, and the Negev Desert to the south.[120]

The geography within these boundaries is called a land of "milk and honey."[121] Historically, this is an allusion to animal husbandry and the use of animal by-products for food and clothing. Goats produced much more milk than sheep, and their skins could be used for a variety of needs. Sheep also produced good wool, as well as food. The designation of honey refers to horticulture as in cultivating fruits and vegetables.[122] Today, the nation of Israel is totally self-sufficient in food. They import no food but export food around the world.

Secondly, the descendants of Abraham were marked to walk in his steps and to inherit the land promised by God.[123] Joseph, with

---

[120] These are, of course, broad estimates. See Genesis 15:18-21.

[121] See Exodus 3:8 and Deuteronomy 31:20.

[122] See the *NRSV Cultural Backgrounds Study Bible* (Grand Rapids, MI: Zondervan Publishing, 2019), 107.

[123] See Genesis 50:24.

his dying breath, made his brothers promise to bring his bones from Egypt to the promised land at some date in the future. It is sad in some ways that the future generations made the covenant all about the land when the land was only a vehicle to support a people beholden to the one-God relationship.

Thirdly, the religious posture I referred to above is called monotheism. This is a really big deal. From all indicators, Abraham was raised in a polytheistic religion of his day.[124] Almost all the ancient gods were tethered to forces of nature. They were worshipped by being flattered, cajoled, humored, and appeased. Manipulation is the operative term to describe the relationship between the devotee and their god.[125] The God of Abraham's covenant is putting to bed all the false ideas about gods of nature developed over centuries by ignorant people and instead revealing Himself as the one true God, i.e., monotheism. This, of course, is done progressively as the covenant unfolds over time. It is the covenant which sets them apart, "revealing their view of history, their belief in destiny; their understanding of the attributes God; their understanding of the obligation to God (in the Torah); and the basis of the prophets institution."[126]

Finally, the result of the covenant: blessing. To understand the full import of the word blessing, we must refer to the concluding verses of Genesis, chapter eleven. You see, the nations of the

---

[124] See Joshua 24:2, 14.
[125] Ibid., Study Bible, 34.
[126] Ibid., Study Bible, 35.

ancient world racked up a track record of rebellion against God so great that God judged them at the Tower of Babel and scattered them throughout the world, severing any former allegiance to self-idolatry. Then in Genesis twelve, God calls a historical figure, who is Abraham to break with the remnants of an idolatrous religion and strike out on a completely new course of devotional life: monotheism. Abraham's obedience to the call of God brought with it a huge life blessing. King David, almost a thousand years later, understood this when he said: "The steps of a man are from the Lord, and he establishes him in whose way he delights; though he fall, he shall not be cast headlong, for the Lord is the stay of his hand."[127]

It's very curious that the word "bless" is used five times in Genesis 12:1-3. A close reading of Genesis chapters 1-11 will reveal the word "curse" is also used five times. Is this a coincidence, or is the covenant with Abraham a reversal of the previous rebellion of humanity?[128] Abraham and his descendants are marked for a missionary assignment. In fact, "Abraham's election is the instrument for the universal purpose of God with the whole world."[129] Israel was designed from the beginning to be a missionary people to rid the world of ignorant unbelief and bring to the fore the truth of the Living God.[130]

---

[127] Psalm 37:23-24.
[128] See Genesis 18:18-19.
[129] Michael W. Goheen, A Light to the Nations: The Missional Church and the Biblical Story (Grand Rapids, MI: Baker Academic, 2011), 31.
[130] See Exodus 19:1-5.

Abraham and the Prophetic

Having been involved in the prophetic for many years, I know how pivotal it is in guiding my steps in ministry. The prophetic, at its base level, is simply "hearing from God." You see, God has created humankind different from all other living things. We are created with a spiritual capacity to commune with the Creator.[131] We can talk to God, and we can hear Him talk to us. As author and friend Dr. Richard Roberts has stated in his new book, *We See in Part: Reframing Prophecy Today*, prophecy consists of "revelation being given to one person in order to be shared with another person or with a group of people."[132] Any supernatural knowledge given to individuals by God qualifies as prophetic.[133]

This is why Abraham's word in Genesis 12:1-3 is so important. Abraham hears from God while a whole new chapter of human history is inaugurated. He is told to leave his country and kindred— his father's house and go. The writer of Hebrews expands on this word:

> "By faith Abraham obeyed when he was called to go out
>
> to a place which he was to receive as an inheritance; and
>
> he went out, not knowing where he was to go. By faith he
>
> sojourned in the land of promise, as in a foreign land,

---

[131] See 1 Corinthians 2.

[132] Richard Roberts, We See in Part: Reframing Prophecy Today, (36 Culverhayes, UK: The Finnian Press), p. 16.

[133] See 1 Samuel 3:10-11; 1 Corinthians 14:1.

living in tents with Isaac and Jacob, heirs with him of

the same promise. For he looked forward to the city

which has foundations, whose builder and maker is God."[134]

By faith, Abraham responded to this word—a word of promise. If he would not have obeyed, he would not have come to the land of promise. This is the way God has always worked with respect to those who would follow Him. God has a plan, but for us to fulfill that plan, it will require the same faith required of Abraham, i.e., obedience to the Word of God, belief in the promise of God.

Here is the caveat. The things in life to which we have a firm emotional attachment are often the things that keep us from entering the full blessing of God. Unless we are prepared to let go, we will never take hold! Unless we move out, we will never move in. God is forever calling us to the next thing. As the book of Hebrews says, "Without faith it is impossible to please him."[135]

So, Abraham picked up stakes and left Ur. He traveled north along the Euphrates River, following the delta green belt, and stopped in the city of Haran, some 700 miles to the north. Haran was a sizable city along an established trade route. It was there that Abraham stayed for some time until his father passed away. Following his father's death, Abraham immediately resumed his journey.[136] Some theologians say Abraham was disobedient and should have never

---

[134] Hebrews 11:8-10.
[135] Hebrews 11:6.
[136] See Genesis 11:31.

gotten waylaid in Haran. I am not convinced that is the case. He was simply honoring his father and mother, which is, by the way, also scriptural. The record speaks for itself. The prophetic spirit would not let him alone. He must resume the journey—and he did. This is the conscience of character. In essence, he was "mugged by reality." He was given an assignment by Almighty God, and he obeyed against all odds.

Abraham journeyed around the Fertile Crecent and landed between Bethel and Ai in the central highlands of Israel. There he pitched his tent and made an altar of sacrifice to God. And throughout the history of Israel, this becomes a "high place" of worship of Yahweh. It was a shrine to the Living God. At Bethel, however, Abraham has not finished his assignment. From there, he journeyed south "in stages" toward the Negev (desert). Most Bibles contain maps of this journey in the back. Check it out.

Abraham Rescues Lot

During the journey south, there came a great famine on the land, which forced Abraham to go to Egypt to live for a period. Upon leaving Egypt, Abraham and his nephew Lot traveled north and decided to separate because the land could not support both of their considerable livestock herds. Lot pitched his tent toward Sodom, a wicked city much like Egypt in character. Abraham, however, journeyed toward the Promised Land and built an altar in Hebron, where he worshipped God.[137]

---

[137] See Acts 7:3-4.

After a period, an Elamite king by the name of Chedorlaomer allied himself with several other kings and attacked the kings of Sodom and Gomorrah and their allies. These kings were more like regional governors and tribal class leaders than kings. However, the Chedorlaomer clan prevailed in battle and ravaged Sodom and Gomorrah. Since Lot was in Sodom, he was taken captive by these invading kings. Eventually, Abraham heard his nephew was captured by the kings and organized a war party of 319 men to rescue Lot. And rescue he did.

Abraham, Mugged by Melchizedek

It is at this point in the narrative that Abraham 's true character shines. The king of Sodom offers Abraham money, goods, and spoils of war for his valiant efforts in saving the day. Abraham could have really made out on this deal, but he declined. Here is what he said:

"But Abraham said to the king of Sodom, 'I have sworn to

the Lord God Most High, maker of heaven and earth,

that I would not take a thread or a sandal-thong or

anything that is yours, lest you should say, I have made

Abram rich.'"[138]

Abraham was looking to the city whose builder and maker is God. It is here Abraham is "mugged by reality" again. His attention is turned toward a mysterious character called Melchizedek, priest

---

[138] Genesis 14: 22-23.

of God Most High. Abraham's encounter with this priest of Salem (Jerusalem) brands an impression on his soul to the point of offering Melchizedek a tenth of everything he had. The book of Hebrews in the New Testament has much to say about Melchizedek as a type and shadow of Jesus Christ. His character far outshines the Levitical priesthood which would come much later in Israel's history. In addition, Melchizedek shares bread and wine with Abraham in a meal together. This obviously is a pre-figuring of Communion.

Please note, Melchizedek has no linage. He just appears. Genealogy is very important to the Hebrew mindset. It helps to track the validity of God working among men and therefore working in history. Family line origins are crucial to this concern. Entire chapters of the Bible recount family lines. Yet with Melchizedek, there is no genealogy, no roots at all. It is a set-up by God. It is a strategic supernatural encounter. This encounter perhaps saved Abraham from leaning into a worldly accommodation with the king of Sodom and thereby avoiding a tragic wrong turn of losing his inheritance of the Promised Land saga. I am sure he was worn out following the battle with Chedorlaomer and could have been vulnerable to a vision collapse. As my friend Leif Hetland says, "There is a battle we fight after the battle we win." Abraham remained strong, refused the offer of worldly pleasure, and went his way strengthened in the Lord. He returned to Hebron and continued in his vision from God.

Summary

My reason for recounting this tedious history is because the entire plan of salvation detailed in the Old Testament record was at stake. I believe Abraham's encounter with Melchizedek was one of the crucial events of all the Old Testament. There are times in our lives when God absolutely calls on us to make a strategic decision. Our destiny lives or falls on such decisions. For example, in the New Testament, God called on Mary to cooperate with the Holy Spirit and have the baby in her womb. Similarly, God called on Joseph to support her and not to cut and run. Yes, God showed up with an angelic influence to tilt them toward the plan, and He will with us as well. When we need to be "mugged," if our hearts are bent toward the Lord, we will be "mugged." These are mysteries that require much prayer and soul searching. In the heat of the battle, our conscience of character will help lead us to a satisfactory conclusion. Our battles may not be as consequential as Abraham's, but they are our battles. Stay close to God. Live in the prophetic and watch the hand of God move in your journey as well.

Finally, remember, following God is as much about timing as it is about direction. God is not in a hurry. There is a timing to the divine movement in our lives. The Hebrew people were in Egypt 450 years. God could have released them at 400 years or 350 years, but he needed a Moses and the backstory of Moses's journey to really solidify the deal. The book of Hebrews says, "Whoever would draw near to God must believe that he exists and that he rewards those who seek him."[139] God has a timing to work his perfect plan. We need the posture and confidence to lean into His good will as we walk out our destined path. We only get one shot at it in this life. Let us make it count.

---

139 Hebrews 11:6.

CHAPTER SEVEN

Jehoshaphat:
Outnumbered and Overwhelmed

In the cataloguing of the lives and exploits of the kings of Israel and Judah recorded in the Old Testament books of Kings and Chronicles, the author interjects a simple phrase indicating whether the king being considered was either a good king or an evil king. It goes something like this: Manasseh did not do what was right in the eyes of the Lord, or Asa did what was right in the eyes of the Lord; Jehoshaphat did what was right in the eyes of the Lord.

With the above designations, the reader gains an immediate evaluation concerning the tenor of the patriarchal reign. However, even when the summary phrase is most positive for the king, we will see that not everything they did was good and right. And yet, the overall big picture of a good king's reign substantiates the long-standing covenant of God with the people. Our king in this chapter, King Jehoshaphat was "mugged by reality" in a dramatic battle with his Moabite and Ammonite adversaries with very unusual results. Before we get the cart before the horse, we need to analyze the ramp-up to the battle with some enduring lessons for us as twenty-first century believers in our journey toward the great consummation of history.

Historical Setting

The period of history we are looking at here is at the close of the tenth century down to the middle of the nineth century B.C. It is a period of sixty-five years during which King Asa served forty-one years, and his son Jehoshaphat reigned twenty-five years. Jehoshaphat is fourth in the lineal decent from Solomon, who was the last king of the United Monarchy. When Asa began his reign, he inherited a time where spirituality was neglected, which, in turn, resulted in a time of social breakdown of the society in general. For example, the Temple was in disrepair, idolatrous worship had crept into the religious system, and obedience to civil law had waned. It was a perilous hour in which the fabric of the kingdom was in jeopardy. The author of Chronicles described it this way: "For a long time Israel was without the true God and without a teaching priest, and without the law.[140] However, a sincere attempt was made to bring restoration to the land. A few verses later, we read:

> "They took oath to the Lord with a loud voice, and
>
> with shouting, and with trumpets and with horns
>
> All Judah inquired with the oath; for they had
>
> sworn with all their heart, and had sought him

---

[140] 2 Chronicles 15:3.

with their whole desire, and he was found by them, and the Lord gave them rest about."[141]

By the time Jehoshaphat took the throne, he was well established in the spiritual formation of his father. His heart was to continue to walk in the ways of the Lord. He brought much prosperity to the nation while being one of the godliest kings to ever sit on the throne. He enjoyed riches in abundance and peace on all sides. So, what is the problem? King Ahab to the north talked Jehoshaphat into a marriage alliance, which eventually led to a military alliance aimed at the region of Ramoth-giliad. This war was a huge mistake. How could a good and great king who had everything going for him make an alliance with perhaps the evilest king to ever sit on the throne of Israel? He was warned by an established prophet not to do it. In the battle, Ahab lost his life, and Jehoshaphat darn near lost his life.

Returning from the battle, Jehoshaphat was met by a man named Jehu, son of Hanani the seer. He immediately confronted the king with these searching words: "Should you help the wicked and love those who hate the Lord?"[142] This word convicted Jehoshaphat and drove him to some real soul-searching and a refocus on all things Jehovah. He appointed judges throughout the land to give "just judgment" among all the people—reinforcing his return to godly rulership. It seemed Jehoshaphat had learned his lesson.

---

[141] 2 Chronicles 15:4.
[142] 2 Chronicles 19:2.

One interesting note to ponder is the repeat factor. Jehoshaphat's father, Asa, did the same thing in his generation: making an unholy alliance with Ben-hadad of Aram (Damascus). The two would pick a fight with King Baasha of Israel. In similar fashion, the two received a scathing prophetic warning from the seer Hanani, Jehu's father, with these searching words: "For the eyes of the Lord run to and fro throughout the whole earth, to show his might in behalf of those whose heart is blameless toward him."[143] The God of heaven is committed not only to get us on the right track in life, but to keep us on the right track. It was a challenge 2800 years ago, and it is still a challenge today. God is concerned with leadership. The people follow the leader; it's just the way it works. If your church or group is not prospering in the Lord, the first place you want to look may be the leadership. Let's do a more recent review.

America's Godly Heritage

Respect for godly principles can clearly be seen during the formation of the American Republic. In 1776, a perfect storm of well-educated Bible-believing leaders set America on a right and godly course in perpetuity because they deferred to the God of the Bible forever enshrined in our founding documents. But how did they get to this point? I am glad you asked! It actually goes back to the people who first landed on our shores: the Pilgrims.

The religious beliefs and institutions the Pilgrims brought with them to New England contributed much to the vigorous free

[143] 2 Chronicles 16:9.

enterprise and democratic form of government we enjoy today. The Pilgrims thought every individual should have a knowledge of Scripture, which meant everyone should be able to read. So, they pioneered in establishing a compulsory system of public education. Education allowed the citizens to be more aware and able to involve themselves in community life.

The Pilgrims believed every individual was equal in the eyes of God, so they made rules, compacts, and institutions that gave each person a voice in the social affairs, including government. These people were deeply religious. Rooted in their belief system was a recognition of God as Creator, Jesus Christ as Savior of the world, and an ardent trust in the imprimatur of the Holy Scripture as our rule for life and society. One can easily see the values present in the colonial experience led to the establishment of a consistent set of social and political institutions. As G.K. Chesterton once observed: "America is the only nation in the world that is founded on a creed." Religious beliefs are interwoven in the creed and reflect its central values of individualism, freedom, and equality. The creed we are referencing is, of course, The Declaration of Independence.

For example, The Declaration of Independence is riddled with a belief in a Sovereign God—who is the judge of the earth and the one to whom we are accountable. The first paragraph invokes the "laws of nature and of nature's God" as the entitlement of the American people to choose separation (from England) as it insists the people have the right to "life, liberty, and the pursuit of happiness." The entitlement comes to us all because the people are "endowed by their creator" to possess these freedoms. In the conclusion, the author appeals to the "Supreme Judge of the world" as he expresses confidence in "the Protection of Divine Providence."

A belief in God as the author of history and the arbiter of nations is deeply entrenched in the conscience of the American Republic. When Abraham Lincoln issued the Emancipation Proclamation in 1862, he appealed to world opinion and to God when he said: "I invoke the considerate judgement of mankind and the gracious favor of Almighty God." When godly leadership throw themselves on the God of history, great and wonderful things can happen. In our story, Asa, and Jehoshaphat could testify to the same.

Jehoshaphat's Back Against the Wall

Circling back to our storyline, Jehoshaphat learned his lesson from the ill-fated alliance with Ben-hadad and got back on track with God. However, sometime later, the warring people of the Moabites and the Ammonites "came against Jehoshaphat for battle."[144] I am sure he must have thought, "Now what?" His heart failed him for fear, yet he set himself to seek the Lord. This was undoubtedly new territory for the king with his back up against the wall and no foreign alliances to confer with. He was alone, outnumbered and overwhelmed. His pensive iteration found in 2 Chronicles 20:5-12 is one of the most beautiful declarations one will read in the Bible. I urge you to read it now.

---

[144] 2 Chronicles 16:9.

Following Jehoshaphat's prayer, a prophetic voice steps in the gap. When I get in a tight spot in life, I often encourage myself with these words from the prophet Jahaziel: "Thus says the Lord to you, do not fear or be dismayed at this great multitude; for the battle is not yours but God's."[145] With these words, Jehoshaphat and all the assembly of Judah bowed their faces to the ground.

Early the next morning, the repercussions of the prophetic word were still reverberating in Jehoshaphat's soul. He appointed those who were to sing and praise the Lord in holy splendor. They actually went before the army singing and declaring Jehovah as their protection to vanquish the enemy. Even though they were outnumbered and overwhelmed, their deliverance was so fantastic, it has gone down in history as one of the most amazing displays of supernatural power ever seen. Somehow, the enemy was completely thrown into confusion and turned on themselves. Jehoshaphat never had to raise a spear. When it was all over, the enemy was dead, and they were alive. It took them three days to gather up all the booty, livestock, good clothing, and precious material articles to take back to Jerusalem.

Should we really be surprised? God told the Hebrews early that as they paid homage to Him and Him alone, He would fight all their battles. Remember: "You will pursue your enemies, and they will fall by the sword before you. Five of you will chase a hundred, and a hundred of you will chase ten thousand, and your enemies will fall

---

[145] 2 Chronicles 20:15.

by the sword before you."[146] The scene has been repeated many times through history, even as recently as June 10, 1967, when a coalition of nations band together[147] to drive the new nation of Israel into the Mediterranean Sea. Israel was so overwhelmed by fire power; unless God intervened, they were sure to drown. And intervene He did! One thing after another happened simultaneously. The tanks of the enemy stalled or got stuck. Their guns jammed, and the troops were in disarray. In this "Six Day's War," as it was called, Israel actually gained more land in the process. It's known as the West Bank, and the Arabs have been whining about it for decades.

The Heavenly Chorus

There is something about the value of praise and worship, about taking the time to get into the presence of the Lord and linger there that completely changes the atmosphere on earth and releases the supernatural abundant power of God over a people. I have personally witnessed this many times in my life. For almost forty years, I led a local church into this kind of atmosphere, and it was an amazing journey, actually, a preview of heaven to come. We used to sing a song entitled "Lord, You Are." The lyrics are as follows:

> "Lord, you are more precious than silver,
>
> Lord, you are more costly than gold;
>
> Lord, you are more beautiful than diamonds,

---

[146] Leviticus 26:8.

[147] Egypt, Jordan, Syria, and Lebanon.

And nothing I desire compares with you."[148]

My church was privileged to have anointed musicians who led us in worship every Sunday without fail. We had a choir that was so anointed, they won first place at the All-Ohio Choir Contest at the Ohio State Fair. Their reward was an all-expense paid professional recorded album of favorite songs. Plain and simple, we had it going on. The church was actually in revival for the entire decade of the 1980s, and we didn't even know it. We held pastors' conferences, renewal weekends for pastors and wives, and special events focusing on national personalities.

On a typical Sunday morning, we would draw people from sixteen different postal zones while we held two morning services and an evening service. Each service was anchored by the Holy Spirit in a United Methodist Church to boot! And it was all because of the heavenly chorus we tagged as "praise and worship" with some decent preaching thrown in for good measure. So yes, I want to close this chapter with some exhortation to the great benefit of praise and worship. It saved Jehoshaphat from a bloody mess, and it will save you as well. This alone is the key ingredient to the local church renewal. Out of its massive influence in my church came evangelism, mission, healing, service to the poor, and much more.

In the early Charismatic Renewal back in the 1970s, we used to sing out of a little spiralbound songbook called *Scripture in Song*. It was simply Scripture verses put to music. Go figure. If it was good

---

[148] Written by Lynn DeShazzo, 1978; Birmingham, Alabama. See http//www.staugustine.com.

enough for King David 3000 years ago, it must be good for us. One of the hallmarks of a true revival is a bursting forth of new music. We witnessed this with John and Charles Wesley in the eighteenth century, and we are seeing it today from all corners of the world. We have sung Vineyard music in the 1970s and 1980s, Hillsong's music in the 1980s and 1990, Gateway music out of Robert Morris's church in Dallas in the 2000s, Bethel music out of Redding California in the 2010s, and Elevation music currently and beyond. God has breathed on the music in our lifetime, and it has affected all corners of the church.[149] I want to unpack the value of praise.

The Value of Praise

Psalm 34 sets the mandate for worship among God's people:

"I will bless the Lord at all times;

his praise shall continually be in my mouth.

My soul makes its boast in the Lord;

let the afflicted hear and be glad.

O magnify the Lord with me,

and let us exalt his name together!"

Praise is the highest order of activity to be found in the lives of men and women. Praise is a form of prayer. It denotes the majesty, the authority, the dominion of Almighty God. Psalm 116:12 asks the

---

[149] *Catholic, Protestant, non-denominational, Pentecostal, and Orthodox.* One would also include Messianic.

question: "What shall I render to the Lord?" The answer: "I will offer to thee the sacrifice of thanksgiving." Old Testament scholar Arthur Weiser weighs in here: "This becomes the surrender of the inner most being of the whole man to God. Evoked and sustained by the love for one who himself has bestowed his own love upon him." There are seven Hebrew words which bespeak the praise of God found in the book of Psalms. They are:

"Halal"- Psalm 113:3: to shine, to make a show, to boast, to celebrate, rave, to be clamorously foolish.

"Thillah"- Psalm 147:1: to sing hallels, to sing praises extravagantly, to celebrate with song.

"Zamar"- Psalm 57:7: to touch the strings (celebrate with song and music).

"Yadah"- Psalm 67:3: to revere or worship (with extended hands).

"Towdah"- Psalm 50:23: to extend the hands, confession, sacrifice of praise, thanks (giving offering).

"Shabach"- Psalm 145:4: to address in a loud tone! Glorify, praise, triumph, shout praise to God.

"Barak"- Psalm 72:15: to kneel, by implication to bless God (adoration).

From this recitation of Psalms, one can draw a few helpful conclusions. First, God dwells in an atmosphere of unceasing praise. His presence and praise have a mutual affinity; where there is adoration, reverence, acceptable worship, there He openly manifests his presence.[150] After all, that which occupies the total time and energies of heaven must find a fitting patter on earth. The church must learn how to praise and why to praise. If heaven considers it important enough to maintain a chorus of praise unceasing day and night, it must be efficacious. The people are called to mirror what God is doing. What we need in our churches is a confederacy of praise, a people who have set themselves on praising and worshipping the Lord God. Engaging in this conscious activity is of the highest order in the universe.

Second, praise is a way of life. David says, "My heart is steadfast, O God, my heart is steadfast! I will sing and make melody!"[151] We must be diligent about this mode of life. The enemy will do anything to keep a church from praising the Lord. I would venture to say, there is more trouble in music and musicians than any other area of the church. I have seen it all too often as I have traveled and preached across the world. We must be wise as serpents and harmless as doves.

Thirdly, our praise is called a sacrifice (Hebrews 13:5). A sacrifice calls for death. In the Old Testament, something had to die to consummate the acceptable sacrifice to the Lord. What must die in our praise is our ego, our judgment, our evaluation of the situation, our opinion. We have all been victims of circumstances and situations which to our judgment seem unfortunate, tragic,

---

[150] See Revelation 4:8; 5:11; 7:9-12; 11:16-19; 19:6.
[151] Psalm 57:7.

calamitous. It is only then that we offer this sacrifice of praise when things are wrong. We die to our evaluations and bless the name of the Lord during trauma. And its power will unfold before our eyes. By the way, we don't praise Him for where we are, but where He is and where He wants us to come and remain.

Finally, a refusal to offer praise in the face of heartache and trauma can lead to self-pity, doubt, fear, anxiety, and distrust. The enemy wants to paralyze us in these things. However, Satan cannot remain where the praise of God is found. Where there is massive, triumphant praise, Satan is bound. Nothing intrinsically evil can come to the trusting child of God.[152] Adversity is meant to leave us strong in the faith and knowledge of God.

So, the response of man to praise God is measured by all seven of the above Hebrew words. As we established a confederacy of praise in my church, it released a culture of praise throughout the entire Body. It actually became a way of life, diligently pursued through a pre-meditated, pre-determined habit of praise and worship. We see this in David's life. He was, for a time, a fugitive from the wrath of King Saul. Saul was jealous of David and became enamored with hate and envy. He pursued David with bitter reproach, cruelty, and subtle scheming. And yet, David encouraged himself in the Lord: "Why are you cast down, O my soul, and why are you disquieted within me? Hope in God; for I shall again praise him, my help and my God."[153]

---

[152] See Psalm 91:9-10.
[153] See Psalm 42:11.

Jehoshaphat made a conscience decision to praise the Lord amid an overwhelming historical circumstance. He responded to the prophetic word given exactly at the right time, and God did the rest. He was "mugged by reality." The unseen realm manifested before their eyes, and God received all the glory. After twenty-five years on the throne, the Bible says, "Jehoshaphat slept with his fathers, and was buried with his fathers in the city of David; and Jehoram his son reigned in his stead."[154]

---

[154] 2 Chroniclers 21:1.

CHAPTER EIGHT

Elisha:
The Pursuit of Passion

Our study of Elisha will cause us to consider the "big picture" of the prophetic in the Bible. As Old Testament scholar James Hoffmeier says, "Defining what a prophet was in ancient Israel is not an easy task as these individuals were engaged on a host of activities, played various roles, used a range of methods of communication, and functioned in different social and religious settings."[155]

In general, the prophetic movement was raised by God to speak to Israel during times of crisis, historical, moral, and spiritual decline. They had in their sights the restoration of the Hebrew people back to their original covenant loyalty. The centrality of the covenant relationship with God established at Mt. Sinai under Moses was always in view here. Saint Peter called them a "peculiar people" in the New Testament. The prophet Amos said, "You only have I known of all the families of the earth."[156] Even Moses records, "If you obey

---

[155] James K. Hoffmeier, The Prophets of Israel; Walking the Ancient Paths (Grand Rapids, MI: Kregel Academic, 2021), 23.

[156] Amos 3:2.

my voice and keep my covenant, you shall be my own possession among all people."[157] In another place, Moses is quoted as saying: "The Lord your God has chosen you out of all the peoples on the face of the earth to be his people, his treasured possession."[158]Israel was like a bride to a groom; they were exclusively bound to the God of history. When God said to the captive Hebrews in bondage in Egypt, "I will take you for my people," the same verb is used for marriage as when a man takes a wife.[159] This is why the Hebrews were held to a higher standard than the other nations of the world.

The Old Testament prophets spoke between 2500 to 3000 years ago, yet they cast a legacy that has continued among the people of God lasting to the present day. The prophets bring revelation from God and deposit it in the soil of contemporary culture. My doctoral mentor, Dr. John Ruthven, said of the prophetic: "It is immediate revelation of the Holy Spirit, resulting in the prophetic word of God delivered into individual hearts."[160]

There are two or three key words which describe the prophetic vein. The first is the Hebrew word *nabiy*, the most common word for a prophet in the Old Testament. It refers to a mouthpiece for God, declaring what the prophet has heard directly from God. For example, when the prophet Balaam was recruited by Balak of Moab to speak a word of curse against the Hebrew people in rout to the Promised Land, Balaam had to retreat and get alone with God first

---

[157] Exodus 19:5.
[158] Deuteronomy 7:6 (NIV).
[159] Hoffmeier, Prophets, p.47.
[160] See Isaiah 59:21.

to hear the word.[161] Some have described this mode of speaking as a kind of "bubbling up" of the word from within. It hits you all at once and just comes out, spontaneously activated by faith.

The other words important to understand in the prophetic are *rach* and *chozeh*. The former means "to see," as in seeing visions, and the latter means "to behold in vision" or "a gazer." These are receptive functions dependent on the manifest presence of God. These people are generally referred to as "seers" in the Old Testament because they "see" the word before they "hear" the word. They may meditate on it for a period and share it at a later date. All true seers are prophets, but not all prophets are seers. Elisha functioned in both as the occasion dictated.[162]

We pick up the story of Elisha at the close of Elijah's life. Elijah's exit from this world is veiled in mystery. Both men were on their way to the Jordan River, where Elijah's journey would end. However, in route, the two seemed to make some strategic stops where companies of prophets lived. Perhaps this was a kind of farewell tour for Elijah before his departure. It seemed that Elijah wanted to die alone, but Elisha would have none of it. At each stop (Bethel, Jericho, Jordan River), Elijah tried to get Elisha to stay back as he traveled to the next point. The famous devotional author Herbert Lockyer says, "It would have pleased the prophet more if no eye had witnessed his whirlwind ride to heaven."[163] And yet, Elisha was

---

[161] See Genesis 20:7; Deuteronomy 34:10; Exodus 7:1; Jeremiah 1:5; Malachi 4:5.

[162] See 1 Samuel 3:19-20; 1 Samuel 9:9, 11.

[163] Herbert Lockyer, All the Books and Chapters of the Bible: *A Combination of Bible Study and Daily Meditation* (Grand Rapids, MI: Zondervan Publishing House), p. 89.

determined to stay by his mentor's side until the final moment.

I want to take note of how important the place of proximity was to Elisha. He was after something—a double portion of inheritance from Elijah. This becomes the pursuit of passion. Scripture tracks those with proximity to great leaders such as Moses at Horeb in proximity to Aaron and Joshua. The Bible is clear the people respected and revered Moses. We also see Samuel in proximity to the school of prophets; we see Solomon's wisdom in proximity to dispute difficult cases of justice. In our story, Elisha knew Elijah had the goods, and he wanted what Elijah had before he left this earth. I believe Elisha wanted that anointing and passion to serve God in his avocation. Proximity is important.

Passion and the Anointing

As the story continues, the final stop at the Jordon River proved to be a destiny for both men. Approaching the water, Elijah took his mantle and struck the water. The water divided, and they crossed. Then Elijah turned to Elisha and asked him: "What may I do for you before I am taken away?"[164] Elisha said, "Please let a double portion of your spirit be upon me." A few steps later, a chariot of fire appeared with horses of fire separating the two men. Elijah went up, but his mantle fell back to earth. Elisha cried, '"My father, my father, the chariots of Israel and its horsemen."[165] Bending down to

[164] 2 Kings 2:9. Please read the entire chapter to get the full impact of that which I have abbreviated above.

[165] The idiom: "*The chariots of Israel and its horseman*" *is used throughout the remainder of the book of Kings to signify the presence of the supernatural invading the natural realm.*

pick up the mantle, he stepped back to the Jordan River and struck the water and must have said: "Where is the God of Elijah?" The water divided, and Elisha crossed back over. Please note, the school of prophets who were watching all this from a distance said, "The spirit of Elijah rests on Elisha and they bowed to the ground before him."

An interesting caveat here pertains to the meaning of the "double portion." Most people think of this as twice the power of Elijah. Actually, Elisha did accomplish twice as many miracles as did Elijah, his mentor. However, the ancient Hebrew protocol for inheritance called for something a bit different. Think of it this way. If a Hebrew father had four sons, he would divide his inheritance into five equal portions. The firstborn son would receive two portions. That is what is in play here.

The NIV translation uses the phrase, "Let me inherit a double portion." This is a signal to Deuteronomy 21:15-17, where the right of the eldest son would receive a double portion. Since Elisha acted as the "eldest son" of Elijah, being his chief disciple; a kind of "prophetic firstborn companion," Elisha is asking to "receive the status of the principal successor of Elijah."[166] He knew his inheritance would not be land or livestock, etc. He had already left all that behind to follow Elijah earlier. He wanted the anointing of his mentor. And that is exactly what he got!

There are three things I want us to consider here in relation

[166] NRSV Cultural Backgrounds Study Bible (Grand Rapids, MI: Zondervan Publishing, 2019), 625.

to the anointing of God. All three are still applicable today. First, the anointing of God is visible. The student prophets "saw" the anointing (mantle) fall on Elisha. When we observe a servant of God ministering in the anointing, there is no question it is real. I have seen it many times in my life. One can see it in action, whether it is healing, the prophetic, tongues with interpretation, or deliverance. It's all visible, observable. For instance, I saw a man with Parkinson's disease, walking with crutches, instantly healed at the Voice of the Apostles conference in October 2022 held in Columbus, Ohio. He threw his crutches aside and ran up to the podium unaided, claiming his healing. No one touched him or prayed for him. Only the Holy Spirit encouraged from the podium.

Secondly, the anointing is transferable. The double portion went from Elijah to Elisha. He knew it, they knew it, and God knew it! We can actually pray for the anointing to be transferred to others who desire to walk in a greater level of power with God. Otherwise, why would the apostle Paul tell the church to "earnestly desire the spiritual gifts, especially that you may prophesy?"[167] Why would Paul tell Timothy to "rekindle the gift of God that is within you through the laying on of my hands?"[168] In addition, God told Moses to set aside Joshua and lay hands on him to transfer the anointing to him so he could take the people into the Promised Land.[169]

---

[167] 1 Corinthians 14:1; Exodus 19:7; Leviticus 8:12; 1 Samuel 9:16.
[168] 2 Timothy 1:6.
[169] See Numbers 27:18-19.

Thirdly, the anointing is actionable. It produces results. When Elisha struck the water, it divided just as it did for his mentor. We must realize the anointing not only highlights a special relationship between God and the anointed vessel, it also carries with it authority and power to rule and work in God's name. God conveys the power and ability to perform the function. Things that were anointed in the Bible include: Jacob's stone pillar; shields for war; buildings such as the Tabernacle in the wilderness; bread, kings, and more. It becomes a mechanism for special resources, for objects, and for people. One Sunday morning in a rented facility in our community while our church was being renovated, we prayed for a twelve-year-old boy who walked with a limp. We sat him in a chair and had him stretch out his legs. One leg was clearly longer than the other. One of my leaders prayed for the leg to be lengthened, and before our eyes, it was lengthened to match the other. From that day on, he was completely healed. I asked a new person attending the church to step behind the curtain on the stage to witness this event. When he saw the leg grow out, he said, "Something snapped in me, and I knew God was real." Later, he became the first elder in my church.

From this point on, Elisha began to minister in his "double portion" anointing. There are too many scenes in the life of Elisha to rehearse to make my point. I will choose the one where Elisha intercedes to thwart an attack on Israel by the Arameans. The episode is found in 2 Kings 6:8-22. Please read the story because I will only list the high points.

In the story, we see the King of Aram decide to attack Israel. However, every time he tried to manufacture an ambush of Israel's troops, he was thwarted. The victims never showed up. Elisha was prophetically warning the troops to avoid such and such a place. The king of Aram was really ticked-off. "How can this keep happening?" he said. One of his officers told him it was the prophet Elisha who tells the king of Israel the words "you speak in your bedchamber." Basically, the king of Aram said, "That did it—let's go get him." And off to Dothan they went—an extraordinary army after one man. Remember the saying in Israel, "one will put a thousand to flight, and two will put ten thousand to flight." Here we go again. An army with chariots and horses surround the city.

When Elisha awoke early the next morning, his servant was in panic mode. Basically, Elisha said, "Cool your jets. Those who are with us are more than those who are with them." Then Elisha prayed that his servants' eyes would be opened to the invisible realm— the realm that is the theme of this book. Low and behold, his eyes were opened to see the mountains surrounding them full of horses and chariots of fire. Elisha prays the invaders would be struck with blindness. They were struck blind in mass. Can you imagine such anointing, and we are still in the Old Testament? Here we are again: "mugged by reality." Elisha proceeds to administer the situation to a peaceful conclusion and without bloodshed. In fact, they ended with a banquet. My word, you've gotta love this guy, Elisha. Please read the conclusion; it is really quite gripping.

The Place of Passion in the People of God

As we are coming in for a landing in this important chapter, I want to discuss what I call the three P's of the prophetic. They are passion, proximity, and purpose. First, passion:

What makes an Abraham radical to obey God?

What makes an Elisha want a double portion?

What makes a Daniel resistant to brainwashing in his Babylonian captivity?

What makes a Moses covet to share the glory of God?

What makes a Mary of Bethany break a vial of pure nard over Jesus, wiping his feet with her hair?

What makes a Roman centurion dare to open his front door to Peter, a Jew?

What makes Priscilla and Aquila risk their lives for the apostle Paul?

Of course, the answer to all these questions is passion. The problem with the church today is there is no passion. The passion has left the building and with it, a much-needed mission conquest. As I write this chapter, we just finished the Superbowl. We all saw Kansas City beat Philadelphia in a squeaker. One of the commercials during the broadcast was sponsored by a Christian group with a solid Christian message: "He Gets Us." One of the principal donors for that seven-million-dollar commercial was David Green, founder of the national chain Hobby Lobby. I presently serve with Mart

Green on the Global Council of Empowered 21, a worldwide council affecting generations for evangelism in the twenty-first century. I can assure you Green's motivation is passion for the Kingdom of God. Think of it—a hundred million people saw that commercial and heard the Good News of God's love in Jesus Christ. That's powerful; that's passion!

The longer I go in ministry, the more I am realizing the need for a passionate walk with God, one that is not motivated by external stimuli because if external stimuli is the determining factor, one will always have to be "propped up" by something from the outside (e.g., music, large crowds, colorful personalities, etc.). However, if internal passion is our motivation, we will be in a place where God can use us most effectively. One cannot read the Psalms without noticing the component of passion at the core of the Psalmist's life:

> "As a heart longs for flowing steams, so longs my soul for thee, O God. My soul thirsts for God, for the living God."[170]

> "O God, thou art my God, I seek thee, my sold thirsts for thee; my flesh faints for thee as in a dry and weary land where no water is."[171]

> "One thing I have asked the Lord, that I will seek after; that I may dwell in the house of the Lord all the days of my life, to behold the beauty of the Lord, and to inquire in his temple."[172]

---

[170] Psalm 42:1-2.

[171] Psalm 63:1.

[172] Psalm 27:4.

"Open my eyes that I may behold wonderous things out of thy law."[173]

The writer had a longing for God's presence, internally motivated. Perhaps this is why the Psalms are so widely read. They reflect something we wish we had. Elisha had Elijah. We have Jesus. I have noticed something about the nature and history of religion. In Christianity, if we fail to focus on the person of Jesus, we will at some point go off the rails by gazing at what I call diversions. What are some of these diversions? Things like: denominations; do-good efforts, which can develop into works righteousness; personalities; local church ministries; theological arguments; political issues, and a host of other things. Please know there is nothing wrong with these things, per se; however, they are a poor substitute for Jesus. That is just the way it is. God wants us to engender a personal passion for Jesus and His Kingdom. When Jesus becomes the love of our life, our life will change and reflect His love. Mike Bickel, the founder of IHOP[174] in Kansas City says, "We have not emphasized Jesus in his magnificent personhood as the focal point of redemption. The church knows Jesus redemptively as Savior, but not intimately as an infinite glorious person." And here is the zinger in all of this, "In many ways, Jesus is still a stranger in his own house."

Proximity

---

[173] Psalm 119:118.
[174] International House of Prayer.

Secondly, proximity is crucial in the pursuit of passion and the prophetic. Jesus chose to spend the last week of His life here on earth in the home of Mary and Martha in Bethany, just a few miles from Jerusalem. I believe their home provided an atmosphere of peace and tranquility. He was among friends who sat at His feet to soak in all they could.

Without warning, Mary gets up and takes a jar of pure nard (costly perfume), which the wealthy used in the preparation of the dead, and broke it over Jesus, anointing his head and feet and wiping his feet with her hair. Everyone was speechless. Mary recognized that Jesus was worthy of all the extravagance she could lavish on Him. She was in proximity to the King, and she wanted to make it count. What would be His reaction? Would He reprimand her, scold her, tell her it was wasteful? There were some present who sharply criticized her for such an action. But Jesus said, "Let her alone, she has done a beautiful thing to me."[175] Funny thing, we are still hearing about Mary. Millions of women have her name. Colleges, hospitals, and more are named after her, while most people cannot even remember the names of the disciples.

One cannot love or have passion for someone they do not know. Mary's affection for Jesus overpowered the normal rules for etiquette. She was all in for the Master. She really got who He was and that propelled her to transgress the cultural boundaries of propriety.

---

[175] Mark 14:6.

I very much want us to see that when we come into His presence in prayer or reading the Word—we are dealing with a real person. He speaks, guides, encourages, reveals, converts, forgives. A cold religious ritualization will never bring us all the way in. John Wesley tried it for years and came up empty. Instead, we must pour our lives out as a drink offering for Jesus and reap the benefit of His might presence in our lives. If we withhold the thing He wants the most—our heart worship, then all the externals in the world don't mean very much.

Purpose

Finally, the third leg of the prophetic chair is purpose. Purpose speaks of goals, direction, achievement, and destination. Where do we want to finally land in our relationship with God? Revelation, chapter four keeps our purpose here on earth in clear perspective. In that chapter, the Apostle John is transported in the spirit to heaven's throne room. The scene emphasizes the stark contrast between heaven and earth; between time and eternity; between good and evil; between illusion and reality, lies and truth, kingdom of light and kingdom of darkness. These are the realities one may see when one peers into the next world.

Reading Revelation is a powerful reminder that this world is passing away. The majesty and eternity of Him who sits on the throne in indescribable splendor completely fill the atmosphere. When our gaze is locked onto that One who has no beginning and no end, only then do we realize our purpose. You see, the picture does not become real when we die and go to heaven; it is real now. Our mission in life is to lock on to heaven's reality—now for us invisible but very real. Think of it; most every mission has a throne room, a kind of seat of operations (e.g., the space shuttle, the Superbowl, government counter espionage, etc.). We should not be surprised Christian mission does as well.

When we discern the throne room of God, our relationship with God goes to a whole new level. The enemy does not want you to know about the throne room. He wants you to think only the "holy elite," the power rangers of Christianity, move in this realm (e.g., trained clergy, experienced apostles, evangelists, etc.). I ask you, was Mary of Bethany a power ranger? No! Was Cornelius in Acts 10 a power ranger? No! Jesus' finished work on the cross makes it possible for weak, broken people to come freely before the throne. God is beckoning us to come to the throne room and walk in His purpose.

So, here is the final thought as we contemplate Mary of Bethany and passion. If we can get where she was, we will be where He is. The place of passion for God awaits in your life. Go there!

CHAPTER NINE

Gideon:
Outnumbered but not Outgunned

As we descend on the story of Gideon in the sixth chapter the book of Judges, we are immediately confronted with the supernatural. Gideon was the son of Joash, the Abiezrite, from the tribe of Manasseh, and the fifth recorded judge of Israel. He lived in a little township known as Ophrah, a few miles east of Bethel. As one encounters Gideon, he is minding his own business, threshing out wheat in the winepress of his father, when the angel of the Lord appeared to him and said: "The Lord is with you, you mighty warrior."[176] This seems to be a rather abrupt and odd thing to say "our of the blue" to a little-known son of Israel. Gideon had no track record to justify such a cameo.

Immediately, Gideon gets on his back fours and challenges this declaration of the angel. Basically, he says to the angel: "If God is with us, then why are we (Israel) over-run and under the thumb of the Midianites?" The angel does not argue. The angel just commissions him to go and defeat the Midianites. Arguing with God

---

[176] Judges 6:12 (NRSV).

may be good therapy for us as humans, but in the end, God wins. We must realize at some point in our journey, when God confronts us with His purpose—He knows more than we do; hence, a forward movement is required. After stating that he (Gideon) is from the weakest clan, while being the least of that clan, the angel reiterates: "I will be with you, and you shall strike down the Midianites, every one of them."[177]

Apparently, accepting the commission from the angel of the Lord, Gideon feels bound to present the angel with an offering of food. After preparing and presenting the offering to the angel, the sacrifice is consumed by the staff of the angel in a millisecond, and all vanishes right before his eyes, including the angel. WOW! That was really something. Gideon must have thought to himself, "Perhaps I am on to something here after all." Later, Gideon decides to start this journey of conquest by pulling down the altars of Baal that belonged to his father and the townspeople. Perhaps this could be a signal to all of us as we journey with the Lord; a good place to start is by eliminating all competing distractions in our life and focus on the task at hand. This Gideon did.

Pulling down the altar of Baal was not a popular thing to do. It enraged the Midianites of the vicinity who then wanted to execute Gideon. Gideon's father intercedes for his son and challenges the rabble with the reasoning that Baal, if a god at all, can defend himself. In fact, some people changed Gideon's name to JERUBBAAL, which means "let Baal contend against him." It appeared that Gideon's

---

[177] Judges 6:16 (NRSV).

commission from the angel was getting some traction after all. Gideon takes his trumpet and begins to call forth opposing forces to battle the Midianites. The trumpet, which we will unpack later, is what we call a "prophetic symbol," used by God to activate His plan and purpose in the earth. In addition, Gideon sends out messengers throughout Israel so he can amass an army to fight and defeat the Midianites on the battlefield.

Gaining Traction

At this point in the story, things are really beginning to heat up. From Gideon's perspective, one more confirmation is required. Gideon puts out a fleece. What in the world is a fleece? Basically, a fleece is a tool to discern the will of God in a particular circumstance. Since the full anointing of Holy Spirit was centuries removed from the biblical scene, the Old Testament personalities had some alternative vehicles to discern the will of God.[178] In fact, various means were used to discern God's perfect will in the Old Testament. For example, a prophet of the Lord could declare the word of the Lord.[179] Sometimes a device known as urim and thummim were used to receive direction for God.[180] However, with Gideon, the fleece was an actual wool rug shorn off an animal.

---

[178] At Pentecost, the Holy Spirit was given in mass to all gathered with open hearts. At that time, everyone who received the Holy Spirit had within them the "decision maker" available 24/7. This literally transformed the believing world and accelerated God's plan of salvation for all of mankind.

[179] See 2 Samuel 12:7-15; 2 Kings 3:15-19.

[180] *A precise determination of these articles of discernment is difficult. They were ornaments on the vesture of the High Priest used to give counsel and direction to Israel at specific points in their journey. See Exodus 28:30 and Deuteronomy 33:8.*

Gideon would lay the fleece on the ground and ask God to soak it with dew during the night, while at the same time keeping the ground around it dry. The following night, Gideon would reverse the process with the fleece dry at sun-up while the ground was wet with dew. Well, it worked in both instances, and Gideon had his answer. OK, here we go—off to war!

Continuing, Gideon's previous call for help materialized into a significant army, i.e., 32,000 foot soldiers showed up on his doorstep. Gideon was way encouraged with this turnout until God upset the applecart. God told Gideon, "You have far too many soldiers for me to get the credit in this battle." Now, I do not know about you, but if there ever was a time to argue with God, this may be the time. How can you have too many soldiers in a battle? One needs firepower in a battle, and 3000 years ago, that translates into "boots on the ground." However, as we said previously, God wins the argument. God tells Gideon to thin the troops by telling them, "Whoever is fearful and trembling, let him return home."[181] At this stroke of genius, 22,000 say goodbye, leaving 10,000 behind.

Gideon thought to himself: "CRAP!" God said to Gideon, "The troops are still too many. Take them down to the water, and I will sift them out there."[182] Gideon must have thought, "You have got to be kidding me!" This was going from bad to worse. But Gideon did as the Lord commanded. Meanwhile, down at the watering hole, a unique thing happened. The Lord designated those soldiers

---

[181] Judges 7:2 (NRSV).
[182] Judges 7:4 (NRSV).

who lapped the water with their hands cupped while they were simultaneously looking out for the enemy as the ones chosen to remain with Gideon. All the others who put their face down into the water to drink freely were dismissed. The number of those troops who lapped the water was 300. The rest, and you can do the math, were allowed to return to their homes. God said, "With the three hundred that lapped I will deliver you and give the Midianites into your hand." [183] So, Gideon had to initiate his campaign with 300 soldiers, while 31,700 returned to their homes. Sometimes, God throws us a curveball because that is precisely what is needed to strike out the batter.

The Battle Plan

Gideon is positioned with his men on an elevated ground, while the Midianites were below in the valley. The Lord God commissioned Gideon to attack the opposing army. Gideon had a weapon no one else possessed—the Spirit of God.[184] However, before engaging the enemy, Gideon was cleared to sneak down to spy on the enemy camp. Stealthily, he approached the camp and listened in on a conversation between two soldiers occupied in the "night-watch" detail. It seems incredulous that Gideon would be in the right place at the right time to hear what he heard. Go figure, you can't make this stuff up. One soldier tells another about a dream he had the night before:[185]

---

[183] Judges 7:7 (NRSV).
[184] See Judges 6:34.
[185] God wants to bring us all to a place where the challenges in our journey are allowed

"I had a dream, and in it a cake of barley bread

tumbled into the camp of Midian, and came

to the tent, and struck it so that it fell: it

turned upside down and the tent collapsed.

And his comrade answered, 'This is no other

than the sword of Gideon son of Joash, a

man of Israel: into his hand God has given

Midian and all the army.'"

Upon hearing this dream, Gideon returned to his camp totally encouraged. He worshipped the Lord and said to the troops: "Get up, for the Lord has given the army of Midian into your hand."[186] He then proceeds to divide his army of 300 into three groups of 100 soldiers each. He gives each man a trumpet and an empty jar with a candle in it. He instructs the men on the ensuing battle plan. They are to surround the camp of the Midianites at strategic spots while at Gideon's signal, they all blow their horns and smash the jars while crying out: "A sword for the Lord and for Gideon."

This action released a terror of fear into the camp of Midian while throwing confusion among the troops. The Midianite soldiers were found scurrying around in the dark, bumping into each other and actually fighting each other as if they were fighting

to "unfold" in God's timing and God's way (Judges 7:15). God allowed Gideon to hear the dream of a Midianite soldier as a sign to him of victory. The key is that he positioned himself to listen. Selah!

[186] Judges 7:15 (NRSV).

the enemy. As the Bible says, "Every man's sword was against his fellow and against all the army."[187] The army fled, and Gideon's men pursued, seizing the confusion to their advantage, and killing those who were left. They captured the two captains whose names were Or'eb and Li'eb, killing them and cutting off their heads. Later, they brought the heads to Gideon, who was beyond the Jordan, as a kind of trophy of war.

Prophetic Symbolism

Earlier, I mentioned Gideon's trumpet as a prophetic symbol. Here, we may want to pay close attention because prophetic symbols point to spiritual depths beyond themselves. A prophetic symbol can be many things common to most people, such as a gesture or an object such as a basket of summer fruit, a song, a piece of art, a river, and much more. For example, Moses's rod was a prophetic symbol of the power of God released to accomplish His will. Gideon's trumpet was a symbol for an activation of divine retribution; the ark of the Covenant was a prophetic symbol of the presence of God among pious followers. The prophet Isaiah went naked and barefoot for three years as a prophetic symbol of those who put their trust in chariots and horses (Egyptians and Ethiopians).[188]

At this point in our study, I would like to alert the reader to the importance of prophetic symbolism along our spiritual journey. It can affect entire groups of people or even nations in their destiny

---

[187] Judges 7:22 (NRSV).
[188] See Isaiah 20:1-6.

through history. Imagine with me five different people lying on the ground, overcome by the presence of God, perhaps in a church service or a large evangelistic gathering.[189] They all happen to experience the same outward manifestation, but inwardly, all five are experiencing a different spiritual phenomenon. The first person is being delivered from a demonic stronghold over their life. As long as the demons are going out and not coming in—it is a good thing. The second person is being healed of a life pain or trauma which has stunted their spiritual development for a very long time. The third person is being touched by the glory and blessing of God just hovering over them like waves of peace and tranquility. The fourth person is faking it because he doesn't not want to be left out. But the fifth person is experiencing a manifestation from God, which translates to a prophetic symbol or statement to the group or being used to address a condition among the people which God desires to rectify.[190] In this illustration, one needs discernment to figure out which one of the five is the greater prophetic symbol.

You see, God desires to manifest Himself among His people. It's a kind of holy bragging, when God can advertise His goodness, His love, His power to heal, as well as His concern for the brokenhearted and the lost. This is nothing new. Read the Bible, study the great revivals of history, and see a consistent pattern of the unusual authenticating power of God in the world. For example, Elisha instructed Joash, the king of Israel, to shoot an arrow out his

---

[189] I personally have witnessed all five examples in ministry over the years.

[190] All five illustrations were used by John Arnott in a conference held in Kansas City in August of 1997 called Passion for Jesus.

window, symbolizing his upcoming victory over his current enemy the Arameans. Elisha told the king he would fight the Arameans until he made an end of them. Elisha instructed the king to take arrows and strike the ground. After three strikes, the prophet rebuked him for stopping prematurely. His future victory could even have been more resounding if he had struck the ground five or six times.[191] There was an anointing on the prophetic symbolism to defeat the Syrian army.

Another example is found in Exodus 17:6, where Moses is instructed to strike the rock at Horeb in the wilderness because the people had no water to drink. The Bible says in the sight of the elders of Israel (i.e., the leaders), he struck the rock with his staff, and the water came forth. Wish I could have been there to see than one! However, the greater prophetic symbolism here is that Christ represents the rock, and the rod of Moses represents the cross upon which Jesus died. Out of the rock great blessings flow to all the peoples of the earth.

Perhaps one of the greatest prophetic symbols is the celebration of the Eucharist or Holy Communion. In Latin, Eucharist is called *sacramentum*,[192] which is akin to an oath of allegiance a soldier would make to a military presence. The Greek equivalent was called *musterion*,[193] from which we get the word "mystery." Link this with what the apostle Paul told the church at Colossae to trust in "the

---

[191] See 2 Kings 13:14ff.
[192] Allan Richardson, ed, *A Dictionary of Christian Theology: Sacrament* (Philadelphia, PA: The Westminster Press), p.300.
[193] Ibid.

mystery of God, namely Christ, in whom are hidden all the treasures of wisdom and knowledge.[194] Please understand, this treasure is not hidden from us; it is hidden for us so we may discover the depths of Christ's love. St. Augustine and St. Thomas Aquinas saw the Eucharist as a sign of holy reality—a means of grace or conduit, a delivery system, if you will, for all the riches of salvation in Christ mediated to those who claim Him as Savior and Lord.

When we take Communion, the invisible grace of God is released in us, changing us, renewing us, and sustaining us in our journey through this dark, fallen world. In its inception, the idea of such a meal was a powerful manifestation that offended great numbers of people, even some of Jesus's disciples.[195] But to those who are being saved, it is the power of God and the life of God. Great revivals in history have broken out during Communion services, including the Scottish Presbyterian Revival known as Cambuslang[196] and the great Barton/Stone Presbyterian Communion service which spawned the Cane Ridge revival in Kentucky in 1801.

The Communion ritual points not only to fellowship with Christ now, but also the rule and reign with Christ in eternity, forever! Who among us could not value such a prophetic symbol? Obviously, we

---

[194] Colossians 2:3, (NIV).

[195] See John chapter 6.

[196] During the Cambuslang Revival of 1747 under the direction of Rev. W. McCulloch, there occurred a series of weeks and months where thousands upon thousands of people observed open-air Communion services while people were saved, healed, and delivered from demonic oppression. The great evangelist George Whitfield preached at many of these open-air meetings as the people came from as far away as Glasgow, Edinburg, and surrounding areas. See UK Wells.org. Accessed 2 April, 2023.

could not put rolling on the floor and Holy Communion in the same category. And yet, both are authentic expressions of the mediation of God to man. Neither could we with laughing, crying, singing, or dancing, yet there is a chapter and verse in the Bible that encourages us to do those very things as expressions of a universal grace. The most wonderful thing of all is what Jesus said: "As often as you do this, do it in remembrance of me." We literally get to repeat the Eucharist hundreds perhaps thousands of times in our lifetime—plumbing the depths of His love. Selah!

Extemporaneous Prophetic Symbolism

A few more personal examples of prophetic symbolism should be sufficient to prime the pump of anticipation for the wonderful manifestation of God in being "mugged by reality." In May 1995, my church moved into a brand-new facility that had been under construction on a thirty-acre plot of land in NE Violet Township, Pickerington, Ohio. It was a thrilling time after relocating the physical plant from across the road, which was landlocked on a quarter of an acre. From a pastor's perspective, the holy grail of a new facility is plenty of parking, regardless of how many people showed up.[197]

Later that month, we celebrated Mother's Day, where the sanctuary was adorned with beautiful mothers from all age groups and dressed to the nines. During the course of our worship, I

---

[197] A one-acre plot of land with four rows of double parking spaces with room for turning lane access will accommodate 150 cars. That is 4350 cars for 29 acres!

discerned God wanted me to call all the mothers up and to prostrate themselves on the floor as a prophetic act symbolizing the value of birthing babies rather than destroying them through abortion. Even though these mothers had put on their Sunday best, many with corsages, the response was huge. I will never forget the lump in my throat before I gave the call: "Lord, are you sure about this?" He said, "I am sure." Up they came, filling the front of the auditorium, the side aisles, and even in the back. There were 517 people in attendance that day. That is a lot of smashed carnations under a willing servant of God. This prophetic act released a powerful spirit over the church that day while the event remained in our collective conscience for years.

Finally, I also remember a seminal event the year before when 60,000 men converged on the ellipse in Washington, D.C. It was a Promise Keepers event, and the National Mall was running with testosterone. At one point in the day, those on the platform instructed us to remove our shoes and kneel for prayer in unison as a prophetic act for spiritual renewal in America. In the wake of a nation in desperate need of revival, this prophetic act of intercession could help spawn social change. The crowd responded in mass, and I have a one-by-four-foot poster to prove it. The very next year, revival broke out in Pensacola, Florida, known as the Brownsville Revival. It lasted several years, and many thousands of young people were rescued from the grip of Satan.

Final Thoughts

Where am I going with this? God is not finished using His powerful tool of prophetic symbolism. Gideon had his trumpet, and he used it under the direction of God as effectively as a Black Hawk helicopter or a Howitzer cannon. Under the direction of the Lord, the most common things can become mighty tools in the hands of those consecrated to God and His kingdom. I believe God has equipped us in our hour of confusion and political confrontation with an unction and a level of power equivalent to the task.

We must, however, keep our eyes on the mark. Many athletic contests result in defeat because the participants fail to execute in the basics. Our basics are prayer, humility, Spirit-led living, speaking the Gospel to everyone in our orbit of life, and standing fast in the face of opposition. Gideon's God is our God. His arm is not shortened that He cannot perform. We stand on the cusp of the greatest outpouring of salvation in the history of the world. One great ingathering awaits a church at prayer. Several large worldwide Christian coalition groups are inaugurating a decade of harvest leading up to 2023—the 2000th anniversary of Jesus Christ's death, resurrection, and Pentecost. I presently serve on the Global Council of one of these efforts.[198] We are just now in the beginning throws of this historymaking decade. There is an awakening coming, but it is on the other side of repentance.[199]

---

[198] See Empowered21.com
[199] See Acts 2:38-39; 3:19.

We all must first repent, change our minds, and walk in the direction of an endtimes mandate. As we are cleansed and recommissioned for perhaps the greatest outpouring of the Holy Spirit in history, let us not miss our appointment with God. Remember: A sword for the Lord and for Gideon!

CHAPTER TEN

David & Bathsheba: Been Here Before

The picture in 2 Samuel 11 is as old as the human race. It is a storyline that even Hollywood would seize upon because it has sex as the central feature. This alone qualifies it for their cinematic presentation.

As the story unfolds, David, King of Israel, is sunning himself on his rooftop (one of my favorite pastimes as well), in the spring of the year, (circa 1000 BC) while his troops are pressing military campaigns in far-off places. One of the central questions most biblical commentators ask at this point is: "Why isn't David with them?" We will get to that later.

Meanwhile, as David is sunning himself, he observes a woman naked and bathing on a rooftop adjacent. The spirit of lust seizes David's vulnerable constitution, and he sends for the women. Directly, she is ushered into the king's presence, and he takes her to bed. With this act of adultery, David plunges his life into a foray of negative events encompassing his life, the lives of others, and the eventual legacy of his kingly leadership.

How could this happen to David? Isn't he the one who wrote most of the Psalms? Isn't he the one who "had a heart after God"? Isn't he the one who God said He would make an everlasting covenant with him and his bloodline? How could this darkness and blight come upon one who demonstrated a record of such loyalty and bravery? After all, he was:

- Called as a shepherd boy and anointed for destiny.

- Single handedly defeated Goliath the giant Philistine.

- Drafted into the King's service (King Saul), only to be intimidated and threatened by the King's jealousy.

- Used his giftedness unselfishly on behalf of the nation and its leaders.

- Refused to kill King Saul, even in self-defense.

- Finally, in a dearth of leadership after Saul's death, did not grab power, but instead, consolidated the nation, defeated the Philistines, conquered Jerusalem, and became its ordained leader.

If for anything else, this story suggests to me that the Bible is a book of authentic material and should be read by every human being on the planet. I say this because the Bible makes no attempt to mask the shortcomings of its heroes. Neither is there any attempt to put the best face forward. Instead, the Bible tells the whole story with all the gory details intact. One can trust in the authority and authenticity of the Bible.

One of the things I noted when reviewing this chapter is how out of character this rendezvous with Bathsheba really was for David. The Spirit of the Lord reminded me of this wisdom: when one is tempted and seized to act in a manner totally out of character for their person, one could be under the influence of demonic spirits—heading toward a threshold of big trouble. I believe it will serve us well to analyze this in greater detail.

Temptation and Sin

First, David was tempted to sin and caved. However, if there ever was an Achilles' heel for most men, it is the lure toward a woman, especially a naked woman. Just ask the pornography industry, which has grown to be one of the biggest industries in the world. Men are hardwired to admire and desire women. David is a living portrayal of this truth. Of course, our Creator knew this from the beginning. It alone would ensure the continuation of the human race. However, with the fall of man in Genesis, chapter three, a whole new set of hazards entered the picture.

Secondly, temptation is a fact of life. It's here to stay. But temptation is not sin. It is the ramp up to sin. David had to deal with it in his life, and we already know it's true for all of us. David's was sex, but perhaps yours is food, pleasure, material things, or a thousand other distractions. Temptation will come—period. It does not mean you are carnal but rather human. That is the way it is.

Thirdly, temptation is rooted in deception. Satan parades something across the horizon of your life and tries to make it look good. Perhaps it is something you need or desire. "With consummate skill the tempter creates a mesmerizing illusion."[200] It doesn't have to be something dark and sinister. It can be a legitimate need—but it is met in an inappropriate way. Satan is the master of half-truth, short view, and immediate gratification. Sometimes, the enemy does have to mask the presentation in order to sell it to us. He knows if we could see sin as it really is, i.e., the result, we would not be so tempted. Consider:

If Lot could have seen the tragedies that would befall him in Sodom, he would not have been so inclined to pitch his tent there, no matter how fertile and well-watered the plain.

If Samson knew that his relationship with Delilah would end in betrayal, blindness, and imprisonment, he would not have gone to her, no matter how beautiful she was.

If David would have known that his affair with Bathsheba would have led to the murder of her husband, the death of his child, and the never-ending turmoil throughout his family and kingdom, he would have avoided it like the plague.

You see the hidden costs of sin unfold gradually, slowly to the bitter end. A Hebrew word that can help us frame this dilemma with sin is the word *akarit*. Bible scholar Michael Brown tells us the word is used sixty-five times in the Old Testament and 20% in the Proverbs. Here is an example: "Listen to advice and accept

---

[200] Richard Exley, noted radio Bible teacher.

instruction, and in the end you will be wise."[201] The *akarit*[202] is that which comes after, or the consequences, the after effects. It's what Satan does not tell you. So, before you sin the next time, remember how you felt after you sinned the last time. The *akarit* can save you much heartache.

And so, the drama of temptation is played out every day all over the world. But God has given us a marvelous gift: choice. We can choose, after surrendering to God; there is a power available to us to choose His way over ours. You see, there is really only one temptation, and it wears many faces. The enemy of our soul knows which face is most appealing to each of us. As per his understanding of our personality, the enemy shapes temptation's face to fit our disposition. But remove the facade and strip away the mask, and it comes down to my will over God's will. We can choose the will of God in almost every situation.

The good news is that as we grow in the Lord and mature in our walk with God, we should expect to leave some temptations behind, both physical and spiritual. God will work with us and help us in this process. The big three will always be there, i.e., the lust of the flesh, the lust of the eyes, and the pride of life,[203] but the power of the Holy Spirit will lead us to alternative conclusion.

---

[201] Proverbs 19:20 (KJV).

[202] Gregory A. Lint, Executive Editor, World Library Press: Proverbs Ecclesiastes Song of Songs (Springfield, MO: World Library Press Inc.), p.176.

[203] 1 John 2:16.

An Interesting Query

Who or what was responsible for the affair between David and Bathsheba? This question has perplexed scholars for many years. Obviously, it was David. However, what other factors were at play? Was it spring fever, boredom, bathing in the open, David acting on his impulses, or perhaps all the above? The scripture specifically says: "In the spring of the year, the time when kings go forth to battle, David sent..."[204] Normally, David would have been with the troops. We all know how David liked a good fight. Some have suggested David was depressed and decided to skip this time of battle. Whatever it was, David was at the wrong place for the wrong time.

In addition, verse four indicates Bathsheba had purified herself from her uncleanness, indicating she was not pregnant by her husband.[205] This would confirm her affair with David produced her pregnancy and birth of an illegitimate son. They both knew it was David's child. To cover his tracks, David had Bathsheba's husband Uzziah placed in the front lines of a current war so he would most likely be killed in battle. The plan worked, and Uzziah was killed. Now, David had two severe sins to deal with: adultery and murder. I say again, search yourself when you are tempted to act out of character.

---

[204] 2 Samuel 11:1.
[205] See Leviticus 15:19-30.

Even though David took Bathsheba as his wife, the consequences lingered. God sent the prophet Nathan to confront David. He told David a story of a rich man and a poor man, whereby the rich man severely took advantage of the poor man. When David seized upon the injustice of the story, Nathan pointed his boney finger at David and said: "Thou art the man." The confrontation cut David to the heart. David was led into a severe introspection, which is recorded in Psalm 32 and Psalm 51. We must say at this point, there is forgiveness of sin, even sexual sin, but the forgiveness does not remove the consequences for the sin, especially sexual sin.

There is no middle ground with sexual activity. It must be used under control. It can devastate and destroy if not kept under control. You either control it, or it will control you. It is a powerful gift, and apart from self-preservation, it remains the strongest motivation in human experience. Many recent, well-documented examples of noted people who have crossed the line with sexual mischief include: Mike Tyson, Magic Johnson, R. Kelley, Bill Clinton, John F. Kennedy, Jimmy Swaggart, Ted Haggard, and scores of others.

I have heard people say, "Well, you can either take it or leave it." Not true! You either have to take it, or you have to leave it. Taking it involves marriage; leaving it involves special giftings and the power of God. You cannot do both. David's choice released a process that not only affected him, but his family, his rulership, and his kingdom for some time to come. It included fratricide, incest, rape, and of course adultery. His sin released a curse on his household:

His son died.

His family suffered public disgrace.

His effective leadership crumbled.

His reputation suffered.

His relationship with God was put on hold.[206]

Was it worth it? Of course not. His separation from the presence of the Lord, that which he treasured above all things, was a rough pill to swallow. Even a cursory reading of the Psalms will betray how much David valued the presence of God in his life.

David's Ace in the Hole

I believe the reason David was able to pull out of his dark corner in which he placed himself was because of his history of pursuing the heart of God through worship. David was a worshipper. Worship was anchored in his being. He instinctively knew if he truly repented, he would be forgiven and could end his days with dignity and hope. As a result, David entered a time of true lamentation.

You might ask: what is lamentation? Is it a ship gone down on the high seas, an old board game gone extinct, or maybe a restaurant gone belly up? Actually, it is the name of one of the books of the Bible. It means "to feel" or " to express grief or sorrow"—often demonstratively. It also can mean "to mourn or wail, express strong regret, and cry with dissatisfaction." Every human being will do

---

[206] See successively: 1 Samuel 2:18; 1 Samuel 22:26; 2 Samuel 15:16; 2 Samuel 22:26; and Psalm 32 & 51.

these things sooner or later. It is one thing to do this because we are upset about our situation in life; it is quite another to do this because we are upset about God's situation, e.g., any condition that breaks the heart of God.

So, King David entered a period of lamentation, self-introspection, and prayer concerning what he had done. Once the baby he and Bathsheba had died, David felt released from the process of repentance. There was no more he could do. God took the baby, and it was time to put the whole sordid mess behind him. His sentiment was: "Can I bring him back again? I shall go to him, but he will not return to me."[207] Simply stated, it was time to move on. David lived out his days with other children born to Bathsheba, including Solomon, who became world famous for his wisdom and the splendor of his kingdom, one of the greatest in all of human history.

How Does One Escape the Tempter's Snare?

1)**To escape the tempter's snare, we must know the truth about sin.** Sin is never without consequences. Ezekiel 18:4 says, "The soul who sins shall die." Galatians 6:7 says, "Do not be deceived, God is not mocked, whatever a man sows, that he will also reap." And Proverbs 6:27 says, "Can a man scoop fire into his lap without his clothes being burned? Can a man walk on hot coals without his feet being scorched.?"

---

[207] 2 Samuel 12:23.

The message here is that if you play with sin, you will be destroyed. It is not worth it in the end—ever! The enemy of our souls does not play fair. He is out to destroy us. If we could just put on wide-angle lens before we plunge into mischief—we may see the *akarit* and avoid the trauma. Michael Brown says, "After the high fades, after the sexual ecstasy is reached, we are left with an empty feeling, a feeling of being unclean, ungratified, discontent." The ancient prophet Jeremiah puts it this way: "For my people have committed two evils; they have forsaken me the fountain of living waters, and hewed out cisterns for themselves, broken cisterns that can hold no water."[208]

2) **To escape the tempter's snare, we must know the truth about ourselves.** We all have a capacity for sin built in from the beginning. Given the right circumstances, we are all capable of unspeakable evil. Only as we acknowledge our weakness, will be find strength in God. David said, "Surely I was sinful at birth. Sinful from the time my mother conceived me."[209] Even way before David's time, the Lord God declared: "The Lord saw that the wickedness of man was great in the earth, and that every imagination of the thoughts of his heart was only evil continually."[210] We are a species in need of God.

3) **To escape the tempter's snare, we must know the truth about God.** The enemy of our soul wants us to think that

---

[208] Jeremiah 2:13.
[209] Psalm 51:5.
[210] Genesis 6:5.

God is hard-hearted, quick to judge, and slow to forgive. Not so. Lamentations says: "The steadfast love of the Lord never ceases, his mercies never come to an end."[211] His love is unconditional. He always stands ready to forgive and redeem, providing the conditions have been met. When we add to this the Psalmist's evaluation, we are secure: "But the steadfast love of the Lord is from everlasting to everlasting upon those who fear him, and his righteousness to children's children."[212]

However, if the enemy cannot convince us that God is hard-hearted, then he will try to make us believe He is a soft-touch and will grant us "special dispensation" because our situation is "unique." Nice try, but no go! God's grace is replete, but if we abuse it, there will be consequences.

4) To escape the tempter's snare, we must know the truth about forgiveness. This part is very simple and straightforward: "If we confess our sins, he is faithful and just, and will forgive our sins and cleanse us from all unrighteousness."[213] In the Communion ritual, we ask forgiveness of every "thought, word, and deed." There is no other name under heaven by which men must be saved. God's offer of pardon is complete in our act of repentance.

5) To escape the tempter's snare, we must know the truth about temptation. Please mark this in your psyche: temptation is not sin. We should not feel guilty for being tempted. If Jesus was

---

[211] Lamentations 3:22.
[212] Psalm 103:17.
[213] 1 John 1:9.

not above it, how can we avoid it? It is a fact of life in a fallen world. We will never escape it. Yet we can pray to minimize it. Matthew's gospel records the Lord's Prayer, wherein we say in part: "Lead us not into temptation."[214] The great apostle Paul said concerning temptation: "No temptation has overtaken you that is not common to man. God is faithful, and he will not let you be tempted beyond your strength, but with the temptation will also provide the way of escape, that you may be able to endure it."[215] When it comes, meet it head on and pray.

6) To escape the tempter's snare, we must know the truth about God's faithfulness. God can actually work in the process of temptation and make it serve His greater purpose of producing spiritual maturity in us.[216] God is our ever-present and our only way of escape. Not a technique, not a theology or ritual, not our age, experience, or anything else. Only God. Rest in this refrain: "And I am sure that he who began a good work in you will bring it to completion at the day of Jesus Christ."[217]

---

[214] Matthew 6:13.
[215] 1 Corinthians 10:13.
[216] See James 1:2-4; 12.
[217] Philippians 1:6.

Concluding Thoughts

David's "mugging" was not a deliverance like all the other examples in this book. It was instead "a wakeup call," which perhaps saved his life and reconstituted his journey to a successful conclusion. And yet, the consequence of his sin remained throughout the remainder of his days. God reached David through the office of a prophet who was used to deliver the truth in the crucible of life.

If it were not for the invisible world of spirituality, nothing would work in this dark, fallen world. But God has invaded our world and left a stigmata to reverse the curse of the law which was sin, poverty, and spiritual death. Yes, the phoenix can rise from the ashes so a positive consequential reality can dominate the end of all things. His name is Jesus Christ. I believe the apostle Peter said it best as he wrote to the exiles in Dispersion: "Without having seen him, you love him; though you do not now see him, you believe in him and rejoice with unutterable and exalted joy. As the outcome of your faith, you obtain the salvation of your souls."[218]

[218] 1 Peter 1:8-9.

CHAPTER ELEVEN

Final Thoughts for the Journey

People today are so conditioned to get their bearings from the physical, empirical world around them, it becomes a challenge to alert them to the reality of the invisible world. Oh, we can entertain the invisible for a brief time, such as a magic show or a *Ghostbusters* movie, but eventually, we must return to our everyday existence where we eat, sleep, work, and play. To convince the average person of the invisible experiences noted in this volume, we first must introduce them to the One who presides over the visible and the invisible: Jesus Christ.[219] Only then can we hope to see them expect the invisible hand of God in their journey.

If this is true, and I believe it is, evangelism is what the Doctor has ordered. I mentioned earlier that I am part of a worldwide effort to launch a decade of evangelism (2023-2033) leading up to the 2000th-year celebration of the death, resurrection, and ascension of Jesus Christ and the birth of the Church at Pentecost. These events were

[219] See Hebrews 1:1-3.

all part of one redemptive expression in history. They are recorded in the Bible, the only book in the world where eyewitnesses bore witness to their experience during these events.

Furthermore, after having watched *The Chosen* series on the life of Jesus Christ, I have pondered on the struggle of the disciples to really believe the Messiah had come in their lifetime and that He recruited them to follow Him. It seemed so fantastic after waiting 2000 years that it would actually unfold on their watch. They struggled with it until Jesus sent word to his cousin John the Baptist in prison, who also was wondering about these things: "Go back and report to John what you have seen and heard: the blind receives their sight, the lame walk, those who have leprosy are cured, the deaf hear, the dead are raised, and the good news is preached to the poor."[220]

It must be equally mystifying to many today to believe Jesus is about to return after 2000 years and to redeem all who believe in Him, while at the same time restoring the creation itself. The ancient prophet Zechariah predicted Jesus would return to the Mount of Olives and walk across the Kidron Valley right through the Eastern Gate of the city of Jerusalem.[221] How can one prepare the world for such an event? Evangelism! The next ten years will prove to be a defining period for the citizens of this green earth. An all-out push is under way to reach every person on the planet with

[220] Luke 7:22-23, NIV.
[221] See Zechariah 14:4. This Eastern Gate is known to history as the "Golden Gate."

the Good News of Jesus' love and forgiveness so every person can have "an authentic encounter with Jesus Christ through the power and presence of the Holy Spirit...by Pentecost 2033."[222]

Reach One

The global network I am part of is a kingdom initiative served by Oral Roberts University, helping to shape the future of the global Spirit-empowered movement throughout the world by focusing on crucial issues facing the movement and connecting generations for intergenerational blessing and impartation. Again, it is called Empowered21. The core of this effort is a personalization of the Great Commission.[223] I want to focus on Mark 16:15: **"Go everywhere and announce the message of God's good news to one and all."**[224]

How important is every person? With COVID-19, every person feels they are to have a platform. Social media has exploded because of our stay-at-home experience. Jesus took time to always go after that one person. Jesus zeroed in on the woman at the well, the man at the Decapolis. Those familiar with the New Testament know the shepherd leaves the ninety-nine to find the lost sheep. The woman finds the lost coin, the wayward son finds his way back home, and on and on. If we take the Great Commission seriously, we will go after the "one." We are all missionaries in plain clothes.

God wants us to develop a sensitivity to the needs of that one

---

[222] Stated vision of Empowered21.
[223] See Matthew 28:16-20; Mark 16:15.
[224] The Message version.

person who intersects our path daily. We are to find people where they are doing life and minister to them the love and power of Christ. For instance, Jesus was in touch when a woman with an issue of blood, having snuck up behind Him and touched the hem of His garment to be healed. **"And Jesus, immediately knowing in Himself that power had gone out of Him, turned around in the crowd and said, 'Who touched My clothes?'"**[225] This happened as Jesus was already on His way to heal Jairus' daughter. His whole life was a series of interruptions, yet He was always focused on Kingdom initiatives—reaching the "one."

I don't believe the church is going to grow by methods and gimmicks or smooth ideas always trying the next new thing. Only as we see ourselves as people with a mandate to share the gospel one on one will the Church advance. I am convinced this is the heart of God in a post-pandemic world.

God's Heart in this Pandemic Atmosphere

How important is every person to the heart of God? If we can reach "one," we can reach the world. I think of Phillip and the Ethiopian eunuch, in Acts 8, who Phillip encountered on the road from Jerusalem to Gaza. This man was overtaken by the Gospel and baptized on the spot. He was ripe, as we say, low-hanging fruit. Since he was part of the queen's entourage, he no doubt took the Gospel to his nation to effect multitudes. Could God be speaking to us to re-personalize or personalize anew the importance of

---

[225] Mark 5:30 (NKJV).

strategic interactions with people? First John 4:17 supplies a focused methodology: **"As He is so are we in this world."** Perhaps it is time to get back to what God's mandate is for reaching the world. Start with the seed, and the one seed will bring a harvest. The Bible says, **"One will put a thousand to flight, two will put ten thousand to flight."**[226]

To frame this, I want us to think of the COVID-19 virus. So small, yet it brought the entire planet to a halt. The post-pandemic world will be moving back into small-group interaction and single-unit importance. If we want to be like Jesus...we must get this. I am talking about a re-calibration of Kingdom method. One size really does fit all. The next generation really needs this truth. A few examples will suffice.

Bobby Grunwald, an entrepreneur and Kingdom strategist trained in Internet Technologies and digital platforms, joined the staff of Life Church in Oklahoma City in 2006. Craig Groeschel is the lead pastor and heads the ARC (Association of Relational Churches). In a two-year period, they birthed two internet platforms: the U-Version of the Bible and Church Online, connecting relationships of people who are geographically dispersed. In 2008, Apple launched their first Apps Store with 200 selections. The two apps developed by Life Church were selected to be in the store. Amazingly, 83,000 people installed it in the first four days. Today, 500 million devices are bookmarking Bible data. Kingdom information is going to reach millions of single online

[226] Deuteronomy 32:30.

recipients. Now we have SoundCloud, Spotify, iCloud, and others to reach people digitally. When the pandemic hit and the doors of the church were closed, digital tools became a window to the world. In 2020, 30,000 churches were using the Church Online app.[227]

In addition, Elon Musk has in recent years launched over 1600 high-speed, low-latency (gigabyte connection), low-orbit satellites. He has a license to launch 35,000. It is called the Starlink Network. In this, the entire Earth will be connected in a way as never before. No matter where you are on earth, you can be connected. This has huge implications for Kingdom of God strategies. You can join Starlink for $100 a month. All this reminds me of the Roman road highway system built by the ancient Romans to carry commerce to Europe and Africa. The early church used these roads to carry the Gospel to the ancient world. Some are still being used today. Could our present-day technology, right here at the end of history, be used to close the Great Commission of Jesus Christ? Think of the possibilities.

The Starlink platform will come down in price as more satellites are launched. The church can leverage new digital platforms today to serve the Kingdom of God and bring in a huge harvest. Efforts are going forth right now to re-personalize the Gospel and reach multitudes via technology.

Finally, many believe we are on the verge of the greatest spiritual harvest of the ages. Multitudes of people are about to be introduced to

[227] As told to the Global Council of E21 in Bogota, Columbia, June 2019.

the Savior of the world. They cannot see Him because He dwells at the right hand of God Almighty. And yet, they will see Him because the invisible will become more real at a point in time than all the material world around them. Stay tuned, my friend; this is going to be an exciting ten years. Shalom.

ABOUT THE AUTHOR

Scott T. Kelso

Scott Kelso ministers in the areas of teaching, preaching, healing and writing, and has a long history of ministering to pastors and their spouses. His deep passion for evangelism and outreach has given him a heart for missions, and Scott has been on missions to Africa, Israel, the Philippines, Mexico, Cuba, and Brazil.

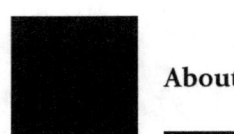

He is a past president of Aldersgate Renewal Ministries in Goodlettsville, Tennessee, a revewal movement in the United Methodist Chruch born in 1977. He presently leads the Five Points-Greater Columbus Apostolic Network, an alliance of churches and ministries gathered to see the Kingdom of God established and maintained in the greater Columbus, Ohio, area. Scott also serves as the President of the Charismatic Leaders Fellowship, an international group of top-tier leaders from all five streams of Christianity (Catholic, Orthodox, Protestant, nondenominational, and Pentecostal) pursuing unity in the Body of Christ. He has been elected to the Jurisdictional and General Conference of the United Methodist Church several times. Scott is the author of *Ice on Fire: A New Day for the 21st Century Church,* published by Thomas Nelson.

Scott earned his Doctor of Ministry degree from United Theological Seminary in Dayton, Ohio, in Supernatural Ministry with the Randy Clark Scholars in 2015. He and his wife Linda live in Pataskala, Ohio. They have three children and seven grandchildren.

FivePoints-GCAN.org

CharismaticLeadersFellowship.org

Books Published by
Scott T. Kelso

- *Theological Violence in the 21st Century: The Exlipse of Ethics and Morality in Today's World* (Boss Media, 2021)

- *The Truth About Grace* (Charisma/E21, 2018)

- *Biblical Eldership: Back to the Future with Spirit Filled Leadership in the Local Church* (Word & Spirit Press, 2016)

- *Let's See What Sticks: Kingdom Living in Chaotic Times* (WinePress Publishers, 2013; Trusted Books, 2014, Second Edition)

- *Ice on Fire: A New Day for the 21st Century Church* (Thomas Nelson Publishers, 2006)

www.ingramcontent.com/pod-product-compliance
Lightning Source LLC
Chambersburg PA
CBHW071405120626
46546CB00002B/824